AD/HD and the College Student

The Everything Guide to Your Most Urgent Questions

AD/HD and the College Student

The Everything Guide to Your
Most Urgent Questions

by Patricia O. Quinn, MD

MAGINATION PRESS ● WASHINGTON, DC

AMERICAN PSYCHOLOGICAL ASSOCIATION

Published by
MAGINATION PRESS
An Educational Publishing Foundation Book
American Psychological Association
750 First Street, NE
Washington, DC 20002

For more information about our books, including a complete catalog,
please write to us, call 1-800-374-2721, or visit our website at
www.maginationpress.com.

Typeset by Circle Graphics, Columbia, MD
Printed by Worzalla, Stevens Point, Wisconsin

Library of Congress Cataloging-in-Publication Data
Quinn, Patricia O.
AD/HD and the college student : the everything guide to your most
urgent questions / by Patricia O. Quinn.
p. cm.
"American Psychological Association."
Summary: "A resource for college students with ADD or ADHD; including
advice on how to design a successful academic program and achieve life-
school balance while managing AD/HD symptoms. Also included
is information on academic accommodations, specialized services,
AD/HD coaching, medication, relationships, and healthy living"
—Provided by publisher.
ISBN 978-1-4338-1131-9 (pbk. : alk. paper) 1. Attention-deficit-disordered
youth—Education (Higher)—United States. 2. Attention-deficit
hyperactivity disorder—United States. 3. Learning disabled—Education
(Higher)—United States. I. American Psychological Association. II. Title.
LC4713.4.Q85 2012
371.94—dc23

2011045873

10 9 8 7 6 5 4 3 2 1

Contents

Contents

Contents

Contents

Contents

Chapter 1
First Things First

Who is Dr. Quinn?

Let me introduce myself. I am a pediatrician with special training in child development and psychopharmacology (treating mental health disorders with medications). I have spent over 35 years diagnosing and treating patients with Attention Deficit Hyperactivity Disorder (AD/HD) and Learning Differences (LD) and am uniquely familiar with how AD/HD can affect you at college. You see, I, too, have AD/HD. After graduating college with a BA in chemistry, I went on to medical school at Georgetown University in Washington, DC. It was there that I learned that I had more problems with studying and some class work than my fellow classmates, but AD/HD in adults was not even a remote possibility to be considered. After my medical internship, I completed a two-year fellowship in child development and in 1972 began conducting research in the area of AD/HD.

Over the years, I have diagnosed and treated many college students with AD/HD, and have also written books on the topic. I have four children, three of whom have AD/HD. They have all graduated from college and two have master's degrees. Since 1997, I have devoted my attention professionally to the issues confronting girls and women with AD/HD, as well as high school and college students with the disorder. I hope that my many years of personal and professional experience will allow me in this guide to answer your questions about AD/HD and provide you with the help you are looking for.

How does this book work?

This guide is written in a question-and-answer format. It is not meant to be read cover to cover. Instead, I hope that you will be encouraged to turn to a section of the book and find answers to your most urgent questions. Dealing with your AD/HD on a daily basis is never a static process. Problems change over time and in a week or so, you may need to come back and re-read a section or look up answers to other questions for problems that have arisen in another area altogether. Whether you are looking for information or dealing with an emergency situation, the table of contents will act as a directory pointing you in the right direction. However, if you are new to an AD/HD diagnosis, you may want to read more than one question or section at a time to get a complete picture.

Throughout this guide, I have used the terminology AD/HD to include all subtypes of AD/HD (Inattentive, Hyperactive, and Combined). I have used learning differences (LD) to refer to general difficulty with learning, unless a particular learning disability like dyslexia or central auditory processing is specifically stated. I have also tried to be inclusive and use the most common names for various services offered on college campuses. However, each institution is different and you may find that your campus uses a slightly different title for the same or a similar service. I have chosen to call the office that deals with students with AD/HD and LD on campus the Disabled Student Services (DSS) office.

Lastly, information contained in this guide should not be considered a substitute for medical or psychological advice and is not intended to replace professional consultation and treatments. Please seek professional help for opinions regarding your particular condition, diagnosis, or treatment.

If you want to read more about AD/HD or related conditions, additional resources such as books, videos, and applications appear in boxes throughout the text.

How can this book help me deal with my AD/HD?

AD/HD is a complex disorder and as such you will need a complex solution to ensure success. Treatment for AD/HD is often described as being multi-modal—comprised of many different components—and encompassing all aspects of daily life. As you will learn in this guide, AD/HD affects your well-being 24 hours a day, 7 days a week, 365 days a year, and can not only affect your academic performance, but also negatively impact relationships, emotions, and day-to-day activities such as eating, sleeping, and getting enough exercise.

This guide will present ways for you to deal with your AD/HD more effectively while attempting to answer your most urgent questions. In order to do this, it will:

Provide information on AD/HD. Gaining a fuller understanding of your AD/HD and its ramifications are important factors in its successful management. While your parents may have pursued this information in the past, as a young adult you will need to take responsibility for your disorder and find out as much as you can for yourself. This guide can help. Pages 9–11 contain a detailed discussion of how AD/HD can affect you at college and what to do about it.

Increase your self-knowledge. The sections on how AD/HD affects you personally, defining your strengths and weaknesses (pages 40–43), and identifying your learning style (pages 43–45) will help you get to know yourself better. Self-knowledge is often the first step to self-advocacy, an important tool for getting what you need to succeed. This is discussed in detail on pages 121–122.

Help you set realistic goals and define ways to achieve them. These two essential tools to future satisfaction in life are discussed on pages 35–38.

Develop your executive functioning (time management and organization) skills. Executive functioning skills (pages 20–21) and other study skills have been found to be critical to success at college. This guide will reveal how working with a coach or academic tutor can help you achieve your goals in these as well as other areas. (See Chapter 10 for more information about AD/HD coaching.)

Help you to maintain good emotional and mental health. This guide includes answers for learning how to deal with stress (pages 53–63) and ways to get the emotional support you need, whether through individual or group therapy or attending peer support groups (page 69). In addition, it will help you learn how to recognize and get treatment for any coexisting conditions such as depression, bipolar disorder, substance abuse, eating disorders, and anxiety (pages 65–68).

Reinforce healthy habits and routines. The lifestyle of most college students does little to reinforce good living habits including eating a nutritionally sound, well-balanced diet with meals spaced evenly throughout the day (pages 79–81); getting enough sleep (pages 73–79); and regular exercise (pages 83–84). Creating a master schedule (pages 132–133) and working with a coach (pages 125–130) can help here as well.

Discuss the medications used to treat AD/HD. It is now widely accepted that medication for AD/HD, particularly stimulant medication, can be one of the most useful tools for reducing the symptoms of AD/HD and improving overall functioning. While medication does not cure AD/HD, combined with other treatments as part of an overall program, it can make a powerful difference in the life of an individual with AD/HD. Specific medications to treat AD/HD are discussed in this guide on pages 88 and 89.

Offer alternative therapies. Many college students make a decision not to take medication for their AD/HD and are looking for alternative ways to address their symptoms. These include diet, meditation, herbal remedies, and supplements. Alternative treatments that have been found to have some scientific merit are discussed on pages 101–105.

Encourage you to investigate specialized help on campus. Specialized services may vary by college, but all should provide supports for basic writing and study skills. In addition, tutors may be available to assist with content in various subjects. Specialized services are discussed in more detail in Chapter 8.

Discuss academic accommodations. The first step in obtaining accommodations that address your needs is knowing what those needs are (see pages 113–115). Second, you'll need to become a forceful self-advocate (pages 121–122). If your college has a well-established disabilities program, and the staff is aware of and has sensitized the faculty to the needs of students with AD/HD, you should have little trouble receiving appropriate accommodations. But, remember, you are the key that opens that door! Most information about accommodations is available in this guide on pages 113–115.

Provide information on AD/HD coaching. Difficulties with time management and planning often interfere with the best intentions of college students with AD/HD. As a result of the problems they have with setting and achieving their goals, overall daily living tasks and academic achievement may suffer. To address these issues, many students with AD/HD hire a

➡ **Extra, Extra!**

For more information about AD/HD and college, check out these books and websites:

Books

Glade, G. *The stimulus driven brain: The essential guide for the ADD/ADHD college student.* Seattle, WA: 5550 Angstrom Press, LLC.

Hallowell, E. and Ratey, J. *Delivered from distraction: Getting the most out of life with Attention Deficit Disorder.* New York, NY: Ballantine Books.

Mooney, J. and Cole, D. *Learning outside the lines.* New York, NY: Fireside.

Moulton Sarkis, S. *Making the grade with ADD: A student's guide to succeeding in college with Attention Deficit Disorder.* Oakland, CA: New Harbinger Publications.

Nadeau, K. *Survival guide for college students with AD/HD or LD.* Washington, DC: Magination Press.

coach. To find out more about how a coach can help students with AD/HD achieve success, see Chapter 10.

Help with choosing a major or career. Counseling around the subject of choosing a major at college is critical for students with AD/HD. Many students with AD/HD have difficulty completing college in four years because they drop courses and change their major repeatedly. They then end up short the required number of

Orenstein, S. *College companion: Your survival guide to college life.* Available as a downloadable pdf at: http://www.addvance.com/bookstore/young.html or on iTunes at: http://itunes.apple.com/us/book/college-companion/id453519079?mt=11

Pappas, P. *One page at a time: Getting through college with AD/HD.*

Sandler, M. *College confidence with ADD.* Naperville, IL: Sourcebooks, Inc.

Websites

http://Addvance.com

http://Help4ADHD.org

http://www.adhdsupport.com/adhd-tips-for-college-students.aspx

http://help4adhd.org/en/education/college/WWK13

http://www.ucc.vt.edu/stdysk/addhandbook.html

http://www.nami.org/Template.cfm?Section=ADHD&Template=/ContentManagement/ContentDisplay.cfm&ContentID=106381

credits in their major for graduation and must take a fifth year to take these courses. In addition, adults with AD/HD often experience job dissatisfaction, and as a result change jobs frequently. To avoid this problem, assessing interests and analyzing career choices to focus on a major field of study in college makes sense. Choosing a major is discussed in this guide on pages 176–178.

Assist you in achieving overall balance in addition to daily structure. As students with AD/HD pursue their college career, they must do so in an environment that is less structured and supportive than the one they experienced in high school. While this opportunity for growth and maturation is a good thing, the student with AD/HD must work to achieve balance and structure on their own. Achieving this balance and structure is discussed in Chapter 11.

Introduce you to an AD/HD-friendly lifestyle. The fact that you have AD/HD may not be under your control, but how you live with your AD/HD is. You can control how you cope with it and how you choose to live. You are the one with the diagnosis and you are the one who needs to make choices and take responsibility for your future. Taking charge of your life and making choices that empower you will allow you to be successful. How to live an AD/HD-friendly lifestyle is discussed in this guide on pages 39–40.

Chapter 2
Understanding How AD/HD Affects Your Life in College

What are the primary symptoms of AD/HD at my age and how might they affect me at college?

Symptoms of AD/HD obviously include problems with attention, concentration, and focus at any age. In addition to these attention deficits, you may also be impulsive (act without thinking through your action or decision), distractible, and/or hyperactive. By the time you get to college, hyperactivity often presents as restlessness, difficulty sitting still for long periods of time, and fidgetiness that can affect sitting through lectures, staying at your designated work space during hours-long science labs, or studying in one place for long periods. You may be disorganized and forgetful or may procrastinate. Problems with time management and completing assignments on time, organizing your schedule, handling your workload, and setting priorities between studying and leisure activities may also be issues and cause you to seem rushed or unprepared. All of these difficulties have a definite impact on academic performance at college, but may also affect leisure activities such as reading a book or watching a movie. Disorganization may cause you to lose things or forget plans with friends. In addition, individuals with AD/HD also tend to suffer from executive function (EF) impairments that cause them to have difficulty with prioritizing, integrating, and regulating other brain functions resulting in problems with learning and getting things done. AD/HD may affect you in other ways. You may become frustrated, have mood swings, and experience difficulty sleeping. Some students may have difficulty completing chores such as doing laundry or other projects and have problems handling their money. College living conditions often compound these problems. You may develop some other secondary symptoms as well. Demoralization, chronic low-level depression, poor self-esteem, and shame may emerge. Your frustration may make you irritable, very sensitive to rejection, and cause negative thinking and self-talk. In addition to these secondary problems, AD/HD is known to coexist with several other conditions. These include mood disorders, anxiety, specific learning disabilities, and obsessive-compulsive disorder. An increased risk of eating disorders has recently been confirmed in women with AD/HD. Of adults with AD/HD, 44 percent have at least one other psychological or psychiatric disorder, 32 percent have two additional diagnoses, and 11 percent have three or more other such conditions (Biederman, et al, 1993).

If you are reading this book, you already know you have AD/HD. Whether you were diagnosed at age 6, 16, or 6 weeks ago, AD/HD is part of your reality at college. In addition to knowing you have AD/HD, there are some other realities that you must be aware of as well. First, you are bright and know how to work hard or you would not have been accepted to college. (However, bright students can fail—particularly if they have AD/HD and other learning challenges!) Second, AD/HD and learning differences, in addition to presenting problems with attention, distractibility, and impulsivity described above, can also impact those areas of your brain that control executive functions and regulate your ability to plan ahead, organize, prioritize, problem-solve, remember what you have to do, and manage time—skills that are critical to college success.

Hopefully, over the last several years, you have come to understand and manage your AD/HD. An uneasy relationship with your AD/HD can sabotage your success and well-being leading to high levels of frustration, stress, and anxiety—feelings which can further hinder your attempts to persevere with academic challenges.

I did well in high school; why is college so difficult for me?

While each student is different, good grades in high school may not be the best predictor of success in college. Often, those grades were earned with a lot of support from various adults in your life, by the structure provided in high school, and the differing academic expectations in high school versus college. In high school, tests are administered on a regular basis and work is usually assigned with a short window for expected completion. That's certainly not the case for most college courses. At college, grades may be made up of only the mid-term and final examination grades or determined by one paper or project assigned for completion by the end of the semester. Your professor at college will most likely not have formal training as a teacher and is often more focused on research or academic content than course work. General undergraduate classes often enroll a large number of students, are held in large lecture halls, and offer little or no opportunity to ask questions.

These unique circumstances along with the executive functioning challenges that accompany AD/HD (problems with time management, memory, and organization) may make the process of achieving academic success more difficult at college, even for those bright students with high IQs who were able to use their intelligence to excel in high school.

A recent study confirmed that while students with high IQs (all had IQ scores within the top 9 percent of the population) and AD/HD also suffered from executive functioning (EF) challenges—difficulty with working memory, processing speed, organization and focus—these impairments did not significantly interfere with their ability to perform well until relatively late in their school years (Brown, et al., 2011). During early school years, many of these students had been placed in special classes or programs for gifted and talented students, only to be removed from these programs as they failed to keep up with work requirements in the more demanding classes. For many, such failures and loss of status caused escalating demoralization as they progressed through their elementary and secondary schooling. A number of the adolescent students with high IQs in this study were not evaluated for AD/HD until their high school years. Half of the students studied were 16 or 17 years old at the time of their first evaluation. Many of these students reported that during elementary school they were able to function in ways that lived up to the high expectations for academic success that were held by their parents, their eachers, and themselves. It was not until secondary school, when they had to keep track of various homework assignments for many different teachers, without anyone to help them to prioritize and remember that AD/HD became apparent in these individuals.

⤤ Extra, Extra!

For more information on this study, visit http://www .drthomasebrown.com.

You may be one of these students and thus have done well in school until the different and multiple demands at college placed pressure on your executive functioning skills and overrode your ability to compensate by using your intelligence and other coping skills.

Right now, if you're feeling that college is tough, you're not alone. In a poll of 2,240 undergraduate students conducted by the Associated Press in 2009, 85 percent of college students reported feeling stressed with worries about grades, schoolwork, money, and relationships. Additionally, 42 percent reported feeling depressed or hopeless and 13 percent showed signs of actual depression. Students with AD/HD are no different and may have even more reasons to be overwhelmed and distressed. College is a unique time and a challenge for everyone. National statistics indicate that five years after starting college, only 55–64 percent of students were still enrolled or had graduated. Of those who had any type of disability, 52 percent were still enrolled or had graduated (NCES, 2000, 2003). While these statistics provide a wake-up call, they should not be a cause for alarm. The good news is that accessing services and resources can help you level the playing field. It has been shown that if students with disabilities accessed support, their graduation rates were the same as their non-disabled peers.

Not all students use available resources, however. Follow-up studies show that only about one-third of the students who received special education services in high school sought formal accommodations in college (Newman, et al., 2009). Keep in mind that getting to college was a big accomplishment, but graduating from college is now your goal. While college is certainly different and in many ways more difficult than high school, there's no reason to think that with hard work and support, you can't succeed in college just like you did in high school. This guide will provide you with information on how to access specialized services and supports, and offer additional resources, such as books, websites, and videos, to ensure your success.

I'm really overwhelmed. How do I know if it's depression, anxiety, my AD/HD, or if I'm just having typical college adjustment problems?

College can at times feel pretty overwhelming for everyone! (See the discussion on page 13.) With independent classwork, mountains of reading and assigned papers, not to mention keeping track of your belongings, living with strangers, taking care of your own needs, and establishing new relationships, the college lifestyle can be pretty stressful for both you and your family. By now, you're probably wondering if AD/HD and college are even compatible at all!

To answer the question of whether you are having more serious issues, you'll need to do a little bit of work, but I can help you get started. First, to see if the problem is just "typical" college adjustment problems, you'll need to get busy. Go out and get some exercise and try not to isolate yourself. If you are a person who has difficulty making friends, or you are shy, or someone for whom new social situations generate a great deal of anxiety, seek out your RA or someone from the welcoming committee on campus. They are usually chosen because they are friendly, easy to talk with, and trained to be helpful. You might ask them to introduce you to someone or make suggestions for ways for you to socialize a bit. Attending a lecture or athletic event can be a way to get out among other students even if you don't have someone else to go with. Talking to others at meals or joining an organization or club that you are interested in may provide a comfortable opportunity for you to meet others and help you feel more like you "belong" on campus. Many first-time, four-year college students (whether freshmen or transfer students) are surprised to find that they have problems adjusting to this new way of living or are homesick, because they had been looking forward to being on their own for so long. It's important to set your mind to work on this problem and see what happens. If you are feeling better about the situation after a few days, it's probably just adjustment issues and your problems will get better over time as you get more comfortable.

Anxiety and depression are completely different issues, however. If after a few days your mood doesn't improve or if things seem to be getting worse, it may be time for professional help. Depression is nothing to be ashamed of. Adjustment to college is difficult for students with AD/HD and they have been found to experience more academic concerns and depression than students without AD/HD (Rabiner et al, 2008).

Separating AD/HD and anxiety may be a little more difficult as these disorders often occur together. It is important to take a serious look at your symptoms, however, in order to determine appropriate treatment options. In general, AD/HD and symptoms of anxiety may be related in one of three ways. First, AD/HD (especially in women) is often accompanied by clinically significant anxiety (as a primary coexisting condition) that may need to be treated in addition to AD/HD. Second, a great deal of anxiety is commonly produced when AD/HD goes untreated (a secondary condition that often resolves as AD/HD is treated and its symptoms become less intrusive); and third, individuals with anxiety may look like they have AD/HD, but, in reality, the poor attention and concentration difficulties they exhibit are directly the result of the anxiety disorder, which needs to be treated. It's therefore extremely important for you to get more information about the signs and symptoms of AD/HD, anxiety, and depression, how each can affect your functioning, and warning signs that you need to get outside help or treatment.

⮑ **Extra, Extra!**

You can check out these sites for more information about depression and a depression screening:

About.com's depression screening: http://depression .about.com/cs/diagnosis/l/bldepscreenquiz.htm

"Depression and College Students," a National Institute of Mental Health publication adapted by UC Berkeley's University Health Services: http://uhs.berkeley.edu/ home/healthtopics/pdf/depresstudents.pdf

"Depression and Anxiety among College Students" on Psychcentral.com: http://psychcentral.com/lib/2008/ depression-and-anxiety-among-college-students/

For more information on anxiety, you can go to:

Anxiety Disorders Association of America: www.adaa .org. There is even an article on anxiety and college students at: http://www.adaa.org/living-with-anxiety/ college-students

The Mayo Clinic: http://www.mayoclinic.com/health/ anxiety/DS01187. The Mayo Clinic's page on anxiety includes a definition, symptoms, risk factors, and more.

AD/HD and how it can affect you at college is the focus of this guide. Clearly, you know that being anxious, or feeling sad, lonely, or hopeless is an issue for you, but how do you decide if you can work on controlling it yourself or whether you need professional help? One way to judge whether you need to seek out help is to look at whether your symptoms are affecting your day-to-day functioning, academic success, or relationships. If you are worried or feel that things are not going as well as you had hoped, go talk with someone who understands AD/HD and how it can impact students at college at the Disabled Student Services (DSS) office or counseling center on campus. What have you got to lose? Only your worry and uncertainty. You deserve to be happy and to enjoy your life, now. Don't let any of these very treatable problems get in the way of those goals.

How do I know if I should see a psychologist, counselor, psychiatrist, or other mental health professional for my problems?

There are several warning signs that the problems you are experiencing need to be addressed by a mental health professional. Recognizing that things at college are not going the way you had planned is the first step. The second step is to determine if the problems you are experiencing are affecting your functioning and significant enough to warrant action on your part. If after reading the following paragraphs, you decide that you need help, take action now. There is no reward in giving a problem more time to see if it gets better. Deciding to get help is a sign of strength! So, find out *now* where the resources are on campus and *go*!

Assess your daily functioning. First, you need to look at whether your problems are affecting your daily functioning and other areas such as eating and sleeping. Are you so anxious or depressed that you can't muster the strength to go to class or out with friends? Would you rather be left alone? Are you sleeping too much? Or are you having problems falling asleep or staying asleep? Are you so anxious that you can't eat? If you have answered "yes" to any of these questions, or have experienced similar thoughts or feelings, it's probably time to get professional help.

Determine if you are self-medicating. Second, if you are beginning to deal with your problems by "self-medicating," it's time to talk to a trained professional. Self-medicating could be defined as using food, alcohol, drugs, or other substances to "stuff down" or "numb out" your emotional pain and discomfort. Seeking temporary refuge from your familiar AD/HD-related problems or new issues that have arisen in the college environment in alcohol or drugs can be a very slippery slope, undermining both your physical and mental health. Ultimately, this substance-use pattern becomes its own problem if it leads to abuse. Substance abuse affects all aspects of a student's life—academic, social, emotional, psychological, and physical. Looking at how you are doing socially and in your course work will let you know if you are in trouble. Waking up with a hangover two or more times a week, skipping class, abusing substances on your own during the day, and isolating yourself are common "red flags" that the situation is out of control. Seeking help early and dealing with your underlying problems are the keys to taking back control of your life. Most campus health or counseling centers have physicians, therapists, and trained counselors to deal with substance use or abuse issues.

Ask yourself if you are feeling hopeless. Lastly, and most importantly, are you feeling hopeless or thinking about hurting yourself? If you ever think about hurting yourself, get help immediately. Visit the campus health center, call an emergency hotline, or go to the nearest hospital emergency room right away. The sooner you start treatment, the sooner you'll be able to manage the feelings that seem overwhelming right now.

⇒ Extra, Extra!

For the National Suicide Prevention Lifeline call 1-800-273-TALK (8255) or visit http://www.suicidepreventionlifeline.org.

Where can I find help on campus?

There are numerous sources of support on campus, but which one you choose depends on the problem you are experiencing. If you are having emotional problems, call or visit the Counseling Center where therapists and numerous programs are available to help you deal with adjustment, depression, anxiety, substance abuse, emotional or other traumas, and eating disorders. In addition to the Counseling Center, you can find help from the staff in your dorm or living center, the University Health Center, and your local health care provider. Clergy and campus chaplains also have experience in helping students deal with many of these same issues and usually have an office on campus.

For problems with your academic program or an individual course, proactively visiting the professor during his office hours (not after a class), contacting your academic advisor, or speaking with someone from a mentoring/tutoring program may quickly resolve the problem. For more general or serious academic issues, make an appointment with the Disabled Student Services (DSS) office or the Office of the Dean of Students; someone there will be able to help you address your specific academic concerns and develop a plan of action. Talking with someone *before* you are in academic difficulty or on probation is not easy, but definitely the best way to handle the situation.

For simpler issues such as adjustment to campus life, getting outside of yourself and connecting with other students is very important. If you talk to other students, you are likely to discover that they share similar questions and concerns. Get out and do something. Getting involved with student organizations and activities are fun ways to interact with other students and get outside of your own head. Meeting people with similar interests can be an exciting way to make friends.

What are executive functioning skills and how could they impact my success?

Executive functioning refers to the tasks performed by the frontal lobes of the brain—the part that is responsible for the skills that you need to pay attention and carry out purposeful activities. In order to get something done, you need to be able to plan, organize, strategize, and hold relevant information in your memory. You also need to be able to "self-regulate"—inhibit inappropriate response tendencies and sustain behavioural output over a long period of time. Subcortical areas and their connection to the prefrontal cortex (executive networks) have also been found to be dysfunctional in people with AD/HD. These striatal/frontal networks are involved not only in attention and focus, but also in cognition, executive functioning, working memory, and motivation. Recent research documents that these brain areas are affected by AD/HD, resulting in poor executive skills and significant functional impairments.

Executive functions develop slowly over the first two decades of life and are thought to manage the brain's cognitive functions (attention, memory, and learning) and provide the "self-regulation" skills discussed above that are needed for daily living. Students with AD/HD and executive dysfunction have problems with processing stimuli, inhibiting control, working memory, and decision making—resulting in the academic difficulties they encounter, sometimes for the first time, at college.

In order to learn new information you need to be able to pay attention, hold the information in your working memory, have a good perception of time, and be able to processes information rapidly. Working memory is the ability to retain, associate, and manipulate information over brief time periods. Working memory allows you to remember what to focus on, recall an instruction, plan and organize an activity, and resist distraction. It has been found that inattention is the best predictor of working memory deficits—independent of age, IQ, and reading/language problems. That is why most students with AD/HD, even the bright ones, have problems with working memory and often experience academic difficulty.

⇨ Extra, Extra!

To read more about executive functioning, AD/HD, and how they can affect your academic success, visit http://www.ldonline.org/article/24880 for the "Executive Function Fact Sheet" by the National Center for Learning Disabilities (NCLD).

What is college usually like for students with AD/HD?

While AD/HD affects every student differently, there are some common issues. AD/HD affects all aspects of life at college—academic, personal, and social. Let's briefly discuss each area here to give you a better idea of how AD/HD might be affecting you. Only then will you know what you can do or what accommodations you need to ask for to improve your current situation.

Academic. Poor organization and time management are major problems for students with AD/HD at the college level and beyond. Frequently it is the very freedom from structured time craved by the college student that ultimately becomes his or her nemesis. Students with AD/HD often become so overwhelmed by the complexity of getting everything done that they become paralyzed and do nothing! Procrastination can lead to "all-nighters" or late assignments. Distractibility can turn writing a paper on the computer into hours spent playing video games or on social networking sites. Reading problems may be the result of not paying attention when you read or from difficulty persevering. Often students with AD/HD find that they have to re-read texts over and over to get the necessary information to answer questions or write an essay or paper. This re-reading takes up a great deal of time, causing them to neglect other subjects or to stay up very late, cutting into the time they would spend relaxing or socializing with friends. As a result of difficulty with auditory processing and the physical act of writing, note taking skills may be impacted. And without good notes it's difficult to study for exams. Writing a paper, because it requires sustained attention and organization of the material, may also not reflect what they have learned or be at the level their professors expect. AD/HD may also affect verbal skills and manifest as inappropriate word choices or word retrieval problems when they are called upon to give a class presentation. Poor verbal skills may also negatively impact their performance during class discussions. These deficits may be further compromised by anxiety or attention problems. In the end, whether a student has one or several of these issues, symptoms of AD/HD often result in academic underachievement.

Personal. As a result of years of struggling with AD/HD, college students often exhibit a high level of frustration and low self-esteem. They may even think that they are not very smart and that the college or university actually made a mistake when admitting them in the first place. Poor grades or the academic difficulties discussed in the section above merely confirm these thoughts and feelings. Confusion about goals and the future may ensue, causing a negative downward spiral. Lack of perseverance or need for immediate gratification may result in their giving up or thinking about dropping out. (If you find that you are having these thoughts, please read the answer to the question about dropping out on pages 162–163.) Their self-care may suffer, even to the point where they aren't showering or wearing clean clothes! Poor time management contributes to all of this as well. Students with AD/HD are working so hard that they don't have time to do it all!

Social. College students will AD/HD may continue to have problems that affect their social functioning. While some students may be very charismatic and easily make friends, they may have more difficulty keeping them. Hyperactivity and/or impulsivity may cause them to overwhelm others, monopolize the conversation, or share more than their listener can handle.

Impulsivity may also result in their doing or saying things that they later regret. Some students with AD/HD may be shy and suffer from social anxiety. They may have problems getting out and meeting other students, a skill that is very necessary at college when away from childhood or high school friends they have known for years.

Although all of these problems may seem daunting, asking questions such as the ones found in this guide and becoming better informed about your options for handling them are important steps towards ensuring a successful outcome to your college career. There is always someone out there to help you find answers or to point to a solution. Remember, self-awareness and a comprehensive treatment program can help you deal with any challenge.

As a young woman, will AD/HD affect me differently?

Women are not only biologically different than men, but neurologically different as well. Studies have documented that in certain areas, the female brain is larger than the male brain. The caudate, hippocampus, and globus pallidus (all areas found deep within the brain) are all disproportionately larger in the female brain, while another midbrain structure, the amygdala has been found to be disproportionately smaller in women. Differences in these structures could explain in part the differing patterns of strengths and weaknesses in women versus men, and might be the cause of variable symptom presentations in certain disorders including AD/HD.

In light of these anatomic differences between the sexes, it would not be surprising to find that women with AD/HD face different struggles and manifest different behaviors than men with the disorder. In addition, women with AD/HD often work harder to conceal their difficulties. They may become perfectionists or develop obsessive-compulsive personalities to overcome forgetfulness and disorganization, or simply spend a great deal of time just getting their work done. Because they typically work harder to hide their academic difficulties and to conform, they often suffer silently, dealing as best they can with their disabilities and the anxiety or chronic low-level depression that accompany them.

Women in general tend to be less hyperactive and more inattentive than men. High IQ, hard work, a supportive environment, a good temperament, and lack of overt hyperactivity or recognizable behavior problems are all factors that may delay AD/HD diagnosis in girls and women. It may not be until college that academic demands begin to exceed your ability to compensate for your inattentiveness, disorganization, and time management issues. This delay in diagnosis may further complicate the picture and impact your performance causing you to seek help for your AD/HD for the first time. For those of you who did well in high school, but who are experiencing problems now, I urge you to read the next question and answer.

I didn't have problems as a girl with AD/HD; why am I suddenly having them now?

As a young girl with AD/HD, you may have found that life was simpler and less demanding and that you were able to compensate for your AD/HD symptoms relatively easily. As opposed to boys, girls with AD/HD often ask for and get help from others (parents, teachers, and tutors) to cope with academic and social demands. In addition, some girls become perfectionists to compensate for their AD/HD symptoms and the lack of control they feel. Girls with AD/HD often make lists or develop habits or rituals (such as lining up their shoes or using certain notebooks) that help them compensate. These strategies allow them to do well in school as long as they live at home and have someone to help them with laundry, making lunches, and shopping, giving them more time to devote to studying.

You may have been successful in high school because you adopted some or all of these strategies. Now at college, you have to do all of these things for yourself, in addition to studying for classes and making new friends. All of this takes time and a great deal of effort. You need to make decisions about which groups to join, who to hang out with, and all the other activities of daily living including when to get up and when to go to bed. You need to get to the cafeteria or shop for and cook your own food, as well as handle money and keep track of finances, again, sometimes for the first time. These extra daily chores and activities, in addition to the increased academic demands of college, place great stress on your time-management and decision-making skills. Often, at this point, the burden becomes too great and young women with AD/HD crumble under the load—either becoming severely depressed or simply overwhelmed and paralyzed—unable to function at all.

If you get help now, you can take steps to develop a program for success and avoid these unnecessary struggles. (See the next chapter for information about designing a program for success.) However, it is essential that you put a program in place whereby you can develop habits, structures, and patterns of living that allow you to balance what needs to be done with your own needs. Without help and support, it is not uncommon for young women with AD/HD to be misdiagnosed with depression or not diagnosed at all, and end up dropping out or being invited to leave college because they could not get it together to function successfully on their own.

Are there any specific scenarios that make things worse at college for students with AD/HD?

Over the years, I have encountered several common pitfalls that can trip-up and intensify problems for college students with AD/HD. In order to help *you* avoid these situations, let's take a look at them now.

Scenario #1. The Instant Cure or Clean Slate Syndrome. Students in this group have had their AD/HD diagnosed and treated for many years. In addition, they have received related services at school and have seen many therapists and tutors along the way. Their parents have been extremely supportive, perhaps even enabling them by taking care of many of their responsibilities for them. When they reach college, however, they feel that no one there will know anything about them and that their disabilities are under control. They now think they have a "clean slate" to begin again without all the fuss of dealing with their AD/HD. So they proceed along without any regard to the many supports and services that had helped them get into college in the first place! "I don't need help anymore!" becomes their mantra. Not taking medications regularly or running out of medication right before exams may be common occurrences, if they take medications at all. Since you must self-disclose your diagnosis at college to receive services, these students go unnoticed until they get in trouble academically.

Scenario #2. The Unrealistic Expectations Syndrome. Students in this group underestimate the amount of time and effort needed to be successful at college. As a result they may err either by taking a course load that's too heavy or not putting in enough effort—cutting classes or procrastinating on assignment work, often trying to complete a semester of reading at the last minute. Regardless of the reason, underestimation of the amount of time needed to complete assignments and poor time management take their toll and these students simply can't get it all done. Stress and poor grades usually follow.

Scenario #3. The Crash and Burn Syndrome. This group also falls victim to poor time management and as a result their sleep and health suffers. Students in this group burn the candle at both ends and may either be up all night studying and then sleep until noon, missing classes and critical information, or they spend too much time partying and having a good time and not enough time getting their work done. Academic performance declines as students in either group suffer the aftermath of their lifestyle choices.

If you saw yourself in one of these scenarios, it's important to take time now to reassess your behaviors and the direction they are taking you. Consider getting help to address your needs, before it is too late and you find yourself on academic probation. Your advisor, coach, or a member of the staff at the Disabled Student Services (DSS) office should be able to help you get back on track. But, you have to seek out and ask for that help. No one is going to just come up and offer it to you.

How involved in my life should my parents be now that I'm in college?

You owe a lot to your parents. After all they have gotten you this far. They probably woke you up in the morning and bailed you out on many evenings or weekends. College is often the first time that you are living away from them. This new independence will require you to learn new ways of interacting with them, and, depending on how much they did for you, there may be several areas of your life that you will need to learn how to manage on your own. By taking the initiative and keeping them informed, rather than waiting for them to question you, you will be able to let them know what you are doing (or planning to do), and even ask for their advice, yet continue to feel like you are in charge. Let's look at several ways you can achieve this balance.

Establish regular check-ins. Don't just call your parents when you need help or money or are sick! First, they probably miss having you around and will want to stay in touch. By setting up a regular check-in time by phone, email, Skype, or texting, you'll feel that you are in control and not that they are interfering in your new life. Be sure to call them to just say, "Hi!" and let them know what you are doing. If you only call to complain or talk about problems, they may think things are worse than they are and feel they need to rescue you.

Set up guidelines for calls. Consider discussing some ground rules with your parents about calls, such as who can call whom, when, and how often. A little planning can avoid too many calls, unfulfilled expectations that may lead to hurt feelings, or calls at inconvenient times.

29

Use them as a resource for your AD/HD. When it comes to managing your AD/HD, they probably know more about you and your disability than you do. So, ask them about what worked in the past, and let them know your plans for dealing with your AD/HD. If you take medication, make sure that you have worked out a way for you to get your medications refilled. Some college students continue to call their parents to get a prescription from their treating physician back home and have their parents refill it and mail the medication to them at college. This system rarely works smoothly. If you waited until the last minute or you have run out of medication, this process can take a long time and you may need to go several days without your medication. Besides, you're the one with AD/HD, and taking responsibility for your own treatment is part of growing up and being on your own. It's best to find a physician locally or in the campus health center who can follow up with you regularly and write prescriptions or make adjustments to your medications as needed. Talking to your parents about this may help you to decide together on a plan that meets your needs.

Take responsibility for your health and medications, but keep them in the loop. If you get sick, contact or go to the health services on campus. Don't call home! Your parents won't be able to do anything for you if you are far away and they will only worry. But, make sure you let your parents know when you are sick and what steps you have taken to be evaluated or to get better, including any medications you are on. You probably are still on their health insurance, and they will get the bills, so you might as well tell them up front what is going on in your life. Show them that you are taking care of yourself and that you can handle your health care responsibly. Make sure you are aware of any allergies to medication that you might have (ask you parents if you need to confirm this important information) and that you have reviewed your immunization records.

Let them know how and what you are doing in your classes. You do owe them—they most likely are paying for your education. One student shared that once he asked his parents to stop asking him about grades and they instead began having discussions about what he was learning in his classes, he enjoyed talking with them. He became interested in what he was learning, and his grades got better! He also discovered that his parents knew a lot more interesting things than he had previously thought!

Discuss money management and your financial responsibilities. It is important to talk with your parents early on about money matters as well as academic performance. Asking them to clarify their expectations about your credit card spending and letting them know about any upcoming special or large expenditures is an important way to stay on the same page and out of trouble. Let them know if you are thinking about getting a part-time job to help out financially. Be sure to point out that it will help keep you on schedule and allow you the freedom of having your own spending money. (See pages 175–176 for a discussion of working while going to college.) Terms of any student loans, including who will be responsible for paying them off and when payments will begin, should also be discussed so that you are aware of any financial obligations you will have upon graduating.

Try to see it their way. Relating to your parents as a young adult is not easy. This whole process is very new for both you and them. They may still think of you as a child. Remember, they have been used to taking care of you for almost 20 years and it's going to be difficult for them to change overnight. There may be some bumps along the way, but you can set the tone by showing them that you are responsible and care about them and their feelings. Because of your AD/HD diagnosis, they have been very involved in your life up to this point, advocating for you and your needs, and it may be difficult for them to hand over the controls. If you reassure them that you are using the many resources on campus and that you know they are right there if you need them for anything, they may be able to relax a bit. You'll be able to stretch and grow some, too.

Without my parents and all of their help, how will I learn to get things done on my own at college?

This is a question that many students with AD/HD never seem to find the answer to at college. Asking this question shows that you realize that you need to develop skills to be successful on your own at college and in life beyond. While it will take some reflection, a little time, and some work on your part, the results will be well worth the effort. Start by thinking about (or maybe even creating a list) of things your parents helped you with in the past (e.g., laundry, getting up in the mornings, scheduling health appointments, and talking with teachers) and decide how you will take on these responsibilities (e.g., develop self-advocacy skills and work on procrastination). Be sure to set realistic goals as you develop these new habits and routines. (See pages 35–38 for more information on setting realistic goals.) An AD/HD coach can definitely help you accomplish these tasks. (See Chapter 10 for more information about coaching and how to find a coach.) Other college resources on campus or in the community may also help you develop new habits and become better equipped to take over these responsibilities. (See Chapter 8 for more information about campus resources.)

Chapter 3
Designing a Program for Success

How can I set goals at college to help me accomplish my dreams for my life, including getting my degree?

This question encompasses a great deal and is one that all college students, not just those with AD/HD, ask themselves. It is also a question that may not have a simple or universal answer, but rather one that is influenced by your life experiences. Students with AD/HD are often confused about the future. Change is difficult for everyone, but may be more difficult if you have AD/HD. Your past experiences may have dampened your enthusiasm about your academic career and your self-esteem may have suffered. In addition, you may want to leave behind being told what to do and simply enjoy being on your own for the first time at college. Setting goals for the future may be the last thing you want to think about. However, in order to be successful at college, you need to know where you are heading and set a course to get there.

At college you will be presented with many opportunities that require both knowledge of your talents, strengths, and weaknesses (to learn more about your strengths and weakness, see the answer to the question on page 40) and a general understanding of the direction you are heading in life. You will eventually need to select a college major and decide on a career path. Asking yourself the following questions may help.

- Where do I see myself five years after graduation?
- What people do I admire? What have they done with their lives?

- What am I passionate about?
- What patterns have emerged in my life up to now?
- When have I done well and been successful?
- When have I struggled and why?
- What fills my time that gives me enjoyment and a sense of satisfaction?

If you still can't decide on your dreams for college and the future, that's okay. Be open and try different things. For students with AD/HD who struggle in various areas it may be overwhelming to think about making all of these decisions at this time. The answers will come as you live life and learn more about dealing with your AD/HD. You don't need to have your whole life planned out or know where you will end up, but you do need to set some realistic, short-term goals in specific areas (i.e. each semester versus all four years at college).

Setting clear, realistic goals for your life, however, isn't as easy as you may think. Typically, people first need to think broadly about what they want to achieve before they pin down a very specific goal. Eventually, they will create a very specific goal to which they commit their time and effort. The more precise and specific you are about what you want to design in your life, the more likely it will be that you will use your conscious thought and energy to deliberately choose what you want to happen. One catchy acronym used often in the workplace and in education for goal setting is the word **SMART**.

SMART goals are:

S = **Specific:** The more detail included in the goal, the better able you will be to focus your efforts. Goals need to state very clearly what you want to accomplish.

M = Measurable: This ties in with the notion of being specific. A **SMART** goal is easy to measure to determine if progress has been made and to establish when the goal has been accomplished.

A = Agreed to: This means that you have committed to taking action and are not complying to make others happy.

R = Realistic: Well-defined goals allow you to believe that you can, with different attitudes and behaviors, take the steps to make change happen. If goals are too easy or too lofty you may lack the motivation to take action.

T = Timely or Time Sensitive: SMART goals state a very specific time frame.

Too often, we never take action because we don't define when we will do something.

For example, if you are not doing well in your Spanish class, you may set a goal to study more to improve your grade. But that wouldn't be SMART. To set a SMART goal you'll need to make the goal measurable (what grade are you aiming for?), and timely (how much more and when will you study?). In addition, just saying that you'll study more may not be realistic or specific enough. First, you'll need to assess why you are having difficulty in the class. If you have a disability that interferes with your learning a foreign language, simply studying more will not do the trick. You may need to arrange for a tutor or join a study group. Let's see how setting a SMART goal would work in this situation.

Problem: I'm doing poorly in Spanish.

Solution (Vague Goal): I'm going to study more.

Solution (SMART Goal):

Specific: I have gotten two Ds on my Spanish tests. I only have two tests left in the semester and I need to pass this class to graduate.

Measurable: I need to get at least a C or higher on these tests.

Agreed to: I really want to pass Spanish now and not have to take the class again in summer school.

Realistic: I took two years of Spanish in high school and got Bs. I know I am capable of passing this class.

Timely: I'm going to attend the Spanish tutorial classes offered by the department twice a week, complete all my assigned work, and study vocabulary for an additional half hour every weeknight.

➥ Extra, Extra!

For help tracking your progress on your SMART goals, check out these sites:

Lifetick: http://www.lifetick.com. Lifetick is web-based software that helps you set SMART goals and track your progress. Lifetick offers free and paid versions and iCal and smartphone integration.

Joe's Goals: http://www.joesgoals.com. Joe's Goals is a simple, free goal tracking website.

42 Goals: http://42goals.com. 42 Goals is another free online goal tracker. A mobile version is available.

StickK: http://stickk.com. StickK is a tool that lets you incentivize achieving your goals in a social way. You set a goal, and if you choose, you can bet money on whether you will achieve it. If you do not achieve your goal, the money that you bet goes to a charity of your choosing.

How can I stop feeling like living with AD/HD is a constant struggle?

Creating an AD/HD-friendly lifestyle will allow you to live with your AD/HD rather than always fighting against it! An AD/HD-friendly lifestyle is one in which you draw on your strengths and let them offset your weaknesses. Living an AD/HD-friendly lifestyle allows you to forgive yourself for past mistakes and use humor to carry you through your present difficulties. It is hard enough to have AD/HD without blaming yourself or being surrounded by family and friends who blame you for your difficulties.

Within an AD/HD-friendly environment, you are also free to practice extreme self-care and to ask for help when you need it without feeling weak or defective. AD/HD-friendly also means an organized lifestyle with easy, convenient places to hang keys, keep papers organized, and store coats, glasses, shoes, sports equipment, backpacks, and books, so that they are not just tossed anywhere and misplaced.

The first step to achieving an AD/HD-friendly lifestyle is looking for stresses in your life that can be reduced or eliminated. Ask yourself, "What gets me off track?" Are you carrying too heavy a course load; taking on responsibilities such as work or activities like pledging for sororities or fraternities your first semester; being too social; or spending too much time on the internet, social networks, or playing video games? An AD/HD brain can get easily overloaded and distracted. It's important that you set an AD/HD-friendly course and then try to stick to it. College isn't just about academics; it's also about learning to live a more balanced life with time to do all that you want to do. It's about having time for what you love and letting your strengths shine and carry you through the dark places.

A second step towards an AD/HD-friendly lifestyle is taking an inventory of friends and associates in your life. You need to consciously seek out people who appreciate your best qualities and are supportive. To make life more AD/HD-friendly, you may need to make an unbiased assessment of the people in your life whose messages are negative and destructive and either educate them about AD/HD or reduce your contact with them. Being around people who appreciate you will allow you to think of yourself more positively and open the way to happiness and success.

⇨ Extra, Extra!

For more information on creating an AD/HD-friendly lifestyle, check out:

Kolberg, J. and Nadeau, K. *ADD-friendly ways to organize your life.* New York, NY: Routledge.

How do I go about determining my strengths and weaknesses?

The best way to discover more about yourself, including your strengths and weakness, is to take some time now to investigate your interests and determine your passions. What do you like to do? What activities or subjects hold your attention? These interests will play a role in your overall college experience, choosing a major, and eventually in your satisfaction with your job and in life. When someone with AD/HD has passion for a topic or a talent in a particular area, there is no holding him or her back. Think about a time when you felt that way about something. What did you accomplish? Did it feel effortless?

We call that functioning in your "green zone." Knowing and working with your strengths (your "green zone") will help you to be successful and stay motivated.

Over the years, you may have spent so much time focusing on your weaknesses and your disabilities that it may be difficult for you to think about your strengths, but everyone has strengths. In fact, knowing your natural talents, skills, abilities, and personal accomplishments will bring you one step closer to understanding yourself, choosing a major, and charting a course to success. Many students with AD/HD may not be aware of their strengths and others may feel uncomfortable talking about them. Some students may even think that they don't have any strengths at all. It is important to begin identifying your strengths and to be able to talk about them with others and to think about how you might use them in a career. Many counselors recommend that you choose a major based on your strengths and interests. (This topic is discussed in more depth on pages 176–177.)

In addition to your natural talents, it is also important to understand that over time various skills can be developed, improved, and turned into strengths. These skills often just require some form of instruction and practice. The point is that you can continue to acquire and build your skills throughout your life. Don't give up on something you love because you don't excel at it now. Your strengths include many things—your skills, natural talents, personal characteristics, and other qualities that make you, well, you! These strengths may include:

- Enthusiasm
- Loyalty
- Honesty

- Humor
- Kindness
- Leadership
- Listening
- Open-mindedness
- Creativity
- Perseverance
- Athletic ability
- Willingness to work hard
- Team player
- Curiosity

It might help you to write down or type up a list of your strengths that you can add to or use whenever you need it. It's also important to know what you enjoy doing, things that you do well, and events or experiences that make you proud and that you feel passionate about. That can be another list.

Sometimes your strengths may be masked by a disability that is not being accommodated, so you may actually think of them as weaknesses. For example, a student who had difficulty with spelling and handwriting when he was younger thought that he was not good at creative writing and would have listed that as one of his weaknesses. As a result, he often avoided classes in which he had to write papers. By using technology and accessing accommodations such as spell-checker, speech-to-text software, and audiobooks, he discovered that he was actually very good at telling a story. His love of learning more about people and his need for stimulation and a constantly changing environment combined to allow him to go on to pursue a career in journalism.

If you are still having difficulty identifying your strengths, try the following:

Review previous report cards. Look at how you did in certain classes to see where you excelled and where you had difficulties.

Go over the reports from previous evaluations. If you have it, review your evaluation from when you were diagnosed with AD/HD. High school IEPs or 504 plans, if you had them, may also point out strengths as well as weaknesses.

Talk with people who know you well. Ask your parents, favorite teachers, and friends to comment on or help you complete a list of your strengths and positive personal traits.

Participate in extracurricular activities. You can learn more about your strengths through personal experiences and activities. By participating in extracurricular activities, community organizations, and volunteer work, particular strengths can be uncovered and further developed.

How do my strengths and weaknesses affect my learning style?

In addition to knowing your strengths and weaknesses, it's also important for you to be aware of your particular learning style and to keep it in mind when selecting classes. Not all people learn the same way. While some experts minimize the effect of learning styles, others suggest that matching teaching and learning styles can enhance learning. Many college students regret not knowing how they learned and studied best before coming to college. It certainly would have made things easier for them and aided in the selection of courses (even majors) and prevented both wasted time and money. Becoming aware of your preferred learning style and where you have problems will make you a more efficient student and can help you minimize stress and frustration.

One of the most common categorizations of the various types of learning styles is the VAK (visual, auditory, kinesthetic or tactile learners) model. Visual learners usually have a preference for seeing; they may think in pictures and benefit from visual aids such as PowerPoint presentations, slides, diagrams, and handouts. Auditory learners best learn through listening; they may prefer lectures, discussions, tapes, and audiobooks. Tactile/kinesthetic learners prefer to learn via experience: moving, touching, and doing. They learn best from active exploration of the world, science projects, and experiments. Students who use this model to identify their preferred learning style can maximize their educational experience by focusing on what benefits them the most.

First, think about these questions:

- How did you study for a test that you did well on in the past?
- What have been your most enjoyable (or effortless) classes in the past?
- Where have you run into difficulty?

Then, ask yourself these questions to help you focus in on your preferred learning style.

- Do you process and retain information better if there are pictures, graphs, charts, and diagrams along with the text? (visual learning)
- Do you process information better if you read aloud, or use audio books? (auditory learning)

- Do you like to be more active and participate in discussion, ask questions, or study with others? (tactile/kinesthetic learning)

- Do you remember what you hear in class or in a lecture? (auditory learning)

- Does writing information down, drawing, or making outlines help you process new information? (visual learning)

- Do you learn by doing or just jumping in and trying to find what works? (tactile/kinesthetic learning)

- Do prefer to have directions explained to you rather than reading them? (auditory learning)

If you would like more information on learning styles in general, check out books on the topic from the library or do an online search. You might also take a learning style survey.

➥ Extra, Extra!

Here are two sites that have learning style surveys that might be helpful:

http://www.personal.psu.edu/bxb11/LSI/LSI.htm

http://www.ldpride.net/learning-style-test.html

Armed with this information, you will be better prepared to take a look at how you should prepare for classes, what accommodations to ask for, and what courses or professors to select.

Chapter 4
Developing Necessary Skills for Succeeding in College

What can I do to make sure I'm succeeding in college on my terms?

Self-determination has been found to be one of the keys to success at college. Self-determination is a concept concerned with supporting our natural tendencies to behave in effective and healthy ways. In order to be successful you need to learn to make AD/HD-friendly choices that support your plan. Sometimes, people with AD/HD are their own worst enemies. The following are some ways to increase your motivation to stick to your plan for success.

Reward yourself. Remember, you are doing this for yourself. So, set up some rewards for when you stay on track. You can only work effectively for so long. Make sure you schedule in some treats and other things that you like to do to keep yourself motivated. Down time is important. Write it in on your master schedule as a reward for when you have completed certain projects.

Look at your motives. Why are you at college? For yourself or for someone else? Do you have a specific career path in mind or are you here because all of your friends were heading off to college and it was expected? You'll be more likely to succeed if you are spending these four years obtaining a degree that allows you to pursue something that you want to do. Career counseling (see pages 109–110) can really help you clarify your motives and choose a major or career path. Check it out! You'll be glad you did.

Work on self-esteem and your emotional state. Significant improvements in students' approach to learning have been seen when self-esteem is improved. In addition, an enhanced sense of overall well-being can result in more positive emotional states, which have been linked by research (Fredrickson & Branigan, 2005) to more effective learning.

How can I improve my executive functioning skills?

Working on your executive functioning is usually a little more difficult, but several approaches can improve these skills as well. The following strategies have been found to be successful in combating executive dysfunction.

Take medication. Taking medication for your AD/HD is probably one of the most important things you can do to improve executive functioning. Medication is one way to normalize brain functioning by regulating the neurotransmitters that contribute to the network dysfunction seen in AD/HD. Medications for treating AD/HD are discussed in depth on pages 87–90.

Improve your goal-setting skills. Students often have difficulty setting and reaching their goals in these areas because goals are vague and unfocused. Learn how to set SMART goals on pages 36–37 of this guide.

Work with a coach. Working with an AD/HD coach has been shown to improve self-regulation, study skills, and determination in studies of college students with AD/HD (Field, et al, 2010). Coaching can also help to build students' confidence and enhance their organizational and time management skills. (For more information on coaching see Chapter 10.)

⮌ **Extra, Extra!**

To read the full report of these studies, go to http://www .edgefoundation.org.

What do I do about my procrastination?

If you have AD/HD, the reality is that procrastination is part of your life. Organization, time management, and difficulty planning ahead will all conspire to make it extremely difficult for you to get work done in advance of deadlines. Even if you have the best of intentions, time after time, distractions or unforeseen delays (like forgetting to get all the material ahead of time) present themselves and hold you back. If it's your strong desire to break the cycle of procrastination, begin by taking a few steps to get you closer to that goal.

Analyze your procrastination. Start with acceptance, then try to get a better understanding of why you procrastinate. First, take a hard look at the reasons you procrastinate.

• Do you have a poor sense of time? Do you find that you consistently don't plan enough time to complete the project before the deadline?

• Do you procrastinate in order to get the stimulation provided by "being under the gun" to get a project done on time?

• Do you enjoy doing things at the last minute?

- Do you like to live in the now and put everything else out of your mind unless it is right in front of you and needs to be worked on now or due the next day?

- Do you have trouble prioritizing what is the most important thing you should be doing right now?

- Does the need to do something perfectly get in the way of you even beginning a project?

- Does anxiety or fear of failure prevent you from beginning or completing projects on time?

Consider your medication. Analyze which symptoms of your AD/HD get in the way the most and investigate whether your medication helps you with those symptoms. If you observe that your medication does help you, make a mental note (or maybe write a post-it note to yourself) to be sure you take your medication when you have work to do. Now that you are more self-aware, it's time to develop a plan that you think will work for you.

Learn to prioritize. Start by looking at what you need to get done now and determine what is the most important or what part will be the most difficult for you to complete. Then schedule a time to work on it. Make sure you write it on your calendar or master schedule. If you tend to become anxious and overwhelmed by a project, working on some of the easier tasks first may give you the confidence to continue.

Divide and conquer. If a large project or a long-term assignment simply overwhelms you, causing you to do nothing until the last minute, try the divide and conquer plan. By breaking the task down into smaller sections with individual due dates, you should be able to complete each task and the whole project on a realistic schedule, ahead of any due date. Just make sure to get the big picture and lay out your plans on a large visible calendar or white board. The bigger the better, so that the plan and due dates are difficult to miss. You might even use different colored pens to call attention to certain dates. With a little bit of insight and the proper planning you will be able to overcome your inertia or fear of failure and gain control of procrastination—even to the point of making it work for you!

If you decide to wait until the last minute, *plan* for it. No guilt or added stress! Just accept that this is who you are and that you can work this way! If you need to use the momentum of working at the last minute on a project—plan for it! Get all the materials ahead of time. Set aside a time and a place and let everybody know your deadline and that you will be working non-stop until the project is finished. Ask that they not disturb you. Shut off the phone and computer and any other distractions. Put a sign on your door. Now that you are ready, *go* for it! Be sure to keep track of time. I'll bet without the guilt and the stress that things will go much smoother.

I'm always late; how can I get to class or appointments on time?

Managing time can be particularly difficult when you have AD/HD. With the many competing demands for your time, it's easy to get off track and overwhelmed. In addition, it has been observed that it is difficult for those with AD/HD to judge the passage of time. As a result, they have difficulty estimating how long something will take, when you should stop in order to move on to the next activity, or how long it will take to get to an appointment or activity on time. All reasons for why you have difficulty being on time.

The second most common reason for not being able to be on time seems to be over-commitment. Taking on one more task (e.g., putting in a load of laundry, listening to one more song, or searching for another shirt) or getting distracted (e.g., stopping at the bookstore or student union) can ruin the best designed morning schedule, and then you find you're late to your first class again! The following strategies may help you get places on time.

Identify what gets you off track in the first place. This technique can be the start to solving this problem. If your problem is the passage of time, wear a watch with an alarm or set up visual reminders (schedules) of what you should be doing and when. If you are distractible, use that to your advantage. Post visual reminders (e.g., signs, post-it notes, or screen savers) in your environment to keep you to a schedule or to remind yourself to stay on track.

Be accountable to someone else. Meeting a classmate and walking to class together can be the incentive you need to get there on time. Call a friend or have them call you to check in to ensure that you are working on what you should be doing or leaving when you need to in order to be on time. If you tend to take on too many tasks in the morning, make a list and stick to it! Don't allow yourself to add one more thing!

Hire a coach. For many students with AD/HD working with a coach empowers them and provides the accountability and structure they need to follow through with their plans.

Set up negative consequences. Try motivating yourself by setting up negative consequences if you are late. Decrease the amount of money you have to spend on entertainment each time you are late or pay money into an account or fund. One girl I worked with had to pay her parents $100 every day she did not get to her first class on time (she had to call them to verify that she was up and in class). She only missed three classes that semester!

Why am I so stressed out?

The key to reducing stress is recognizing that you are stressed in the first place. Once you identify that you are feeling stressed, you will be better able to take a look at the main cause(s), assess the effects stress is having on you, and develop a plan to deal with it. Stress is only a symptom that something is not going as it should, and that your life is unbalanced. Let's look at some of the main stressors at college for students with AD/HD. Over the years, I have often heard students with AD/HD say, "I forgot I had a test (or that the paper was due), so I had to pull an all-nighter." Forgetfulness, disorganization, over-commitment, not getting enough sleep, not learning from your mistakes or looking at the consequences of your behaviors can all contribute to the development of physical and emotional stress. Continuously operating in your "red zone," a place that emphasizes and relies on your weaker skills, can create stress as you become worn down by constantly struggling or over-compensating for your AD/HD.

Identify negative cycling. Stress can set up a negative cycle making it more difficult to pay attention and function effectively. Being under constant stress also places a drain on your energy reserves and physical and mental well-being, making you more susceptible to getting sick or depressed. Some people respond to increased stress by bingeing or having trouble eating. Others experience an increase in anxiety or difficulty falling asleep.

Challenge your ideas about good and bad stress. While some students are negatively affected by stress, others use stress and the adrenaline rush that accompanies it as a motivational tool. These students use the pressure of going up against a deadline to get their work done. Are you one of them? If you are, watch out! Your AD/HD can cause this plan to backfire as you run out of time (poor time management) or get sidetracked (distractibility), causing grades to suffer as you are forced to turn in less than your best effort. Lack of awareness of your own limits or an inability to set appropriate boundaries on your time (common characteristics in those with AD/HD) can make this plan even more risky.

Can stress be beneficial?

Stress is not something anyone can get rid of completely. Stress, managed well, however, can work for you. It may alert you that something is wrong or needs to change, or provide the motivation to change, thus becoming a useful tool for moving you from your "red zone" to your "green zone." Remember, stress is something to manage, rather than struggle against. Too much pressure to make stress "go away" can be very, well, stressful! Take a minute now and try to identify what is causing your stress, the symptoms of AD/HD that may be contributing to your stress, and any effects that stress may have on you (for example, trouble sleeping, eating too much, or bad grades). It might be helpful to write this information down somewhere you can refer to it later and adjust it as you begin to manage your stress.

How can I reduce my stress?

After you have identified some of your main stressors, you can work on dealing with and reducing your stress level in general.

Develop healthy habits. Healthy habits can help you to build up your energy reserves and make it less likely that you will be drained by stress. Taking care of yourself may sound simple, but it is actually harder to accomplish than it sounds. It means getting eight hours of sleep on most nights, eating three nutritious meals a day, drinking lots of water, and exercising regularly. To accomplish this level of self-care, you'll need a plan. Here are some ideas.

Meals. To avoid skipping meals or going too long without eating, enroll in a meal plan, or have enough food on hand in your room or apartment, and set alarms on your phone or watch as reminders to eat. Making a "date" to meet with a group of friends for meals may help you to stop what you are doing and take time to eat.

Sleep. Getting enough sleep is usually a bigger problem. College life is at total odds with good sleep patterns. Pinpointing the reasons you are not getting to bed at night is often the first step in figuring out a plan for getting more sleep. Once you have determined how much sleep you need, decide on a time for lights out, and identify what would need to happen earlier in the day or evening for you to be ready to turn the lights out at this time. Some students find it helpful to set an alarm on a cell phone to go off each night an hour before the time they identified. Examine your nighttime routine and determine when you should finish studying to get to bed on time. Decide if it would help to have some down time, like reading or listening to music, right before lights out; whether you should leave your cell phone somewhere other than in the bedroom so you won't be tempted to text your friends late into the night; and if you should you turn off your laptop or disable access to social networking sites at a scheduled time. Many sleep researchers agree that it's a good idea to stop looking at backlit screens at least a half hour before lights out to help improve the quality of sleep.

Exercise.   Develop a "no excuses" attitude when it comes to exercise. There is a great deal of evidence about the positive effects of exercise on reducing stress, anxiety, and depression. Even short bursts of exercise, such as throwing a Frisbee, taking a 10-minute walk, or doing some jumping jacks, lunges, squats, or push-ups, have been shown to reduce stress. So don't let anything stop you! Join a team, enroll in a class, or enlist an exercise buddy if you need the extra motivation!

Plan ahead.   If you know that certain situations are stressful for you—for example, writing papers—try to set up a plan ahead of time to get this accomplished with the least amount of stress. Typical strategies include canceling any extracurricular activities or obligations around those dates. Decide on a schedule and a place to get your work done and try to stick to it. Be on your guard as you work, and take a break, exercise, or take a nap if you feel stress starting to build. Not being caught off guard by stress can be a powerful way to make it more manageable.

Listen to your body.   Take a few minutes right now and try to identify what happens to your body when you get stressed. Do you clench your jaw? Bite your nails? Tighten your back and develop a backache? Get an upset stomach? These "tells" are your body's way of warning you that you are under stress. Be on guard for these signs of stress. If you feel any of them, be sure to immediately take measures to avoid letting the stress build.

Operate in your "green zone."   This means trying to accomplish tasks by using your strengths to help you live well day to day. As a student with AD/HD, you may have operated for years feeling that academics and learning were difficult for you. Trying to pay attention and stay seated for extended periods, getting things done on time, and organizing your work may have felt impossible. That's because you were operating in your "red zone" or areas of weakness where your AD/HD symptoms have their greatest impact.

At college, you will have more freedom and opportunities to choose how you will live. Instead of always trying to conform to the way others are doing things, it's important that you begin to define your areas of strength and use them to carry you through these difficult tasks. For example, let your creativity help you find alternative solutions to problems and your stubbornness and perseverance see you through to the end. You can now choose lively discussion classes, held in the evening when you are more alert, and avoid sitting through long lectures with hundreds of other students. If you have lots of energy and exercise helps you concentrate, you can go for a run in the middle of the day between classes or labs. It also means giving yourself permission to use accommodations such as dictation software or listening to books on tape when trying to write papers or complete reading assignments. Taking advantage of your strengths will make completing difficult tasks easier and can greatly reduce your feeling of stress.

Use visual imagery to reset mental stress. This can be a powerful tool. Start by creating a visual image of how you feel when you are stressed. Then, create an image of how you feel when you are calm. Try to actually feel it! The next time you realize you are becoming stressed or out of control, take a minute and call up that feeling of inner calm. Sometimes, it helps to think of an actual or imaginary place that you particularly enjoy and where you feel peaceful. A quiet beach, lying in a hammock with palm trees rustling overhead? Skiing alone down a mountain trail in the cool, crisp morning air? Sitting by a stream or next to a quiet pool of water? Whenever you feel your body getting tense, take a few minutes and visit your calm oasis. It's kind of like taking a mini-vacation. You can also achieve the same effect by framing a picture or hanging a poster of your favorite spot, activity, or happy situation, and spending some time looking at it when things get tense or you feel overwhelmed.

Try deep breathing. When things get overwhelming, you can reduce stress in the moment by stopping and taking a few deep breaths. Try this: breathe in slowly to the count of eight, hold it for the count of four, and then breathe out slowly to the count of eight. After doing this slow, deep breathing three or four times, don't you immediately feel calmer? You can practice this quick stress-buster anywhere, anytime for a quick reprieve from feeling stressed, but remember, you still need to address the issues that are causing you to be overwhelmed in the first place.

Practice meditation. Meditation combines slow breathing and relaxation and is a great way to clear your mind as you focus on your breathing. It can be very helpful, especially when you are stressed or feeling out of control. During meditation, you use oxygen more efficiently, your heart rate and breathing slow down, your blood pressure normalizes, you produce fewer stress hormones and your immune function improves. Meditation as a treatment for those with AD/HD is still a new area of research, but has produced some promising results (Black, et al., 2009).

However, your AD/HD symptoms (short attention span, distractibility, and difficulty focusing) may make it more difficult for you to clear your mind and focus, as your inner thoughts or external sounds may keep jumping in and interrupting. Meditation can be difficult for many people to learn, so don't get frustrated if it takes time for you to develop. Keep in mind that there are many ways to meditate. Meditation can be done sitting, walking, or lying down. Doing it your way—the way that helps you the most, not necessarily the "perfect" way—is what you are aiming for. The following is one way to meditate. You may want to conduct an internet search to find out about others like Transcendental Meditation (TM).

- Begin by sitting or lying comfortably on the floor or on a pillow.

- Place your hands in your lap or at your sides.

- Close your eyes.

- Breathe in and out slowly and evenly.

- Breathe in and count one.

- Breathe out to the count of two.

- Keep doing this until you reach 20.

- After you get to 20, keep breathing slowly and try to be very still. Think about things that make you happy, or just let your mind wander.

- After a few minutes, take a deep breath in and out to end the meditation.

- Next, stand up and stretch, feeling relaxed and calm.

It may take some time before you can do this exercise well, but if you are interested in learning meditation, you can work with someone who teaches these techniques to help you improve. These days, many college campuses offer meditation classes or extracurricular sessions, so students can easily access guided meditation led by practitioners.

Try progressive muscle relaxation. Progressive muscle relaxation is a great way to help get rid of stress, calm yourself when you are angry, and quiet your mind. It's a little bit more difficult than deep breathing, but well worth the effort. If you have trouble settling down during the day or falling asleep at night, try the following exercise as a way to relax or de-stress. By tightening and relaxing the muscles in every part of your body, you can release stress and feel calmer. You'll be able to relax any time you want by following these simple steps:

- Start by lying down on your back, on your bed or the floor, with your eyes closed.

- Tense (tighten) the muscles in your toes and feet as hard as you can by curling your toes under.

- Hold this tightening while counting to 10 slowly.

- Then release and relax these muscles. Lie quietly for one or two minutes.

- Next tense your calves (backs of your lower legs) by pointing your toes while counting to 10.

- Relax for a few minutes.

- Now tense or tighten the muscles in your legs while counting to 10.

- Relax and lie quietly for a few minutes.

- Now tighten the muscles in your stomach while counting to 10.

- Relax on your back for one or two minutes.

- Continue this tightening and relaxing with all the muscle groups in your hands, arms shoulders, neck, and face.

After tensing each group of muscles, remember to hold the tightness to the count of ten. Then relax the muscle group for a few minutes.

When you are finished with this exercise, lie quietly with your eyes closed and breathe slowly in and out for a while. Listen to your breathing and hold on to this relaxed feeling.

Try brain wave training to induce relaxation/stress reduction. Have you heard of this technique for relaxation, stress reduction, or falling asleep? It is based on the scientific study of particular brain wave patterns that are seen when a person is engaged in these various activities. This technique involves listening to music with embedded beats that induce the brain to adopt certain patterns depending on the state that is desired. Binaural beats allow you to set frequencies that are then embedded in music for sleep, relaxation, and concentration.

⤴ Extra, Extra!

Multiple apps are available with different combinations and music to choose from. I have listed a few of the programs here, but you'll be able to find others as well.

100 Binaural Beats: http://itunes.apple.com/us/app/100-binaural-beats-isochronic/id369912947?mt=8. $0.99, compatible with the iPhone, iPod Touch, and iPad.

iRelax melodies: http://irelax-melodies-sleep-meditation-yoga-relaxation.soft32.com. Free, compatible with the iPhone and iPod.

Ambiance 1000: http://ambiance.urbanapps.com. Free, compatible with desktop, iPhone, iPod, iPad, Android.

Seek out campus resources. It does appear that there is some connection between a student's perception of available help and his or her stress level. Students who use learning services and academic support to help manage their AD/HD-related issues tend to experience lower levels of both stress and substance abuse. Consequently, knowing the resources on your campus and using them is critical. Remember, you or your parents are paying for them! (Campus resources are discussed in more detail in Chapter 8.)

Develop your plan. It can be useful to have a plan in writing. Write down some ideas of how you might deal with and reduce your stress. In addition to using some of the stress-busters above, consider whether you need to seek professional help to better control your AD/HD symptoms or deal with anxiety or depression caused by your stress-filled situation. (See the next chapter for information about emotional support.)

Chapter 5
Seeking Emotional Support

Should I tell anyone about my problems, feelings, or the help I'm getting?

Students who find they are having problems with adjustment, anxiety, depression, or substance abuse often feel that they are the only ones experiencing difficulty and that everyone else is just sailing through this transition or difficult time. You may have been caught off guard. You may have been so looking forward to college and getting away and being on your own that you never expected or planned to get homesick or anxious. Emotional traumas, issues with roommates, and romantic relationships must now be faced in a new setting without the comfort of home or long-time, best friends. However, the longer you wait to do something or to talk with someone about how you are feeling, the more likely you are to encounter negative feedback from others about your mood or behaviors, and to increase the negative feelings you have about yourself. Waiting usually makes things worse, not better. More intense negative feelings only result in more intense emotional pain.

Many college students confess that they don't want to talk with other students or tell their parents what is going on because they feel that they should be on their own and handling these issues themselves. They think that telling anyone about their problems or talking about their feelings would be a sign of weakness. In fact, just the opposite is the case! So often it is in the process of talking about your feelings and problems that you'll find that others may be feeling exactly the same way, but, they, too, were afraid to talk about them. It is also important to remember that your parents only want what is best for you. You are not asking them to rescue you, but to listen and be a source of support while you seek help.

How do you find the right person to talk with about your feelings or problems with stress, drugs, or alcohol? If you are living on campus, you might start with the Resident Assistant (RA) assigned to your floor or dorm building. They are trained to deal with these issues and know what resources are available on campus. You might also look up an older student, someone you feel close to. Maybe you have something in common—same home town, high school, or athletic interests. Don't be afraid to email or call your parents. Just make sure that you let them know that you are calling to keep in touch and to report on how things are going, and not because you expect or want them to rescue you. Rehearse what you are going to talk about with them and also let them know about the steps you have already taken to get help.

But above all, be patient! You'll find that over time things will get better if you work at connecting with others and are not afraid to get the help you need.

Who should I talk with about my AD/HD?

The staff at the Disabled Student Services office should always be your first stop at college for any issues regarding your AD/HD diagnosis. Service providers are trained to help students deal with AD/HD and its consequences. In addition, your academic advisor may be able to help, depending on experiences he or she has had with other students with AD/HD. You may also seek out other students to talk with to combat common feelings associated with AD/HD—isolation, stress, frustration—but it is important to be somewhat discriminating in whom you choose. Students with AD/HD should be cautious and not impulsively share their diagnosis with just anyone. Often they find that other students may see them as having an unfair advantage because of their academic accommodations and question the need for them. You may also want to be cautious about disclosing that you take medication for your AD/HD in order to avoid being asked to share it with others. (See pages 98–100 for a more in-depth discussion of these issues.)

Are there any other supports that will help me deal with my AD/HD and related emotional issues?

College students with AD/HD may need individual psycho-therapy sessions with a therapist to deal with individual stress-ors. Many students with AD/HD typically develop a chronic sense of being a failure because they are unable to meet the demands of daily life, leading to low self-esteem and chronic low levels of depression (dysthymia), issues which may need to be addressed in individual psychotherapy sessions.

By young adulthood, many persons with AD/HD have become very down on themselves. They incorporate past experiences and failures or words that they have heard from others into unhelpful thought patterns that say they can't accomplish much and that they will always be failures. When they fail at something or when things don't work out as expected, they feel that it only further confirms what they have been telling themselves all along.

But this does not need to be the case. AD/HD-focused cognitive behavioral therapies (CBT) that cover a broad range of issues including self-esteem, relationship and family issues, daily health habits, stress level, and life management skills—all issues where medication alone has either little effect or takes a great deal of time to make a difference—are reported by mental health professionals to have a significant impact on their patients with AD/HD (Ramsay & Rostain, 2005). In general, CBT challenges the ingrained unhelpful patterns of thinking seen in individuals with AD/HD and encourages alternative patterns of thinking that reassure them that the outcomes of events in their life are under their control and that they can make healthy changes. After learning new ways to talk to themselves, statements like "I'm good in math" or "People do like me!" can go a long way towards helping these students make academic progress or establish new friendships.

In addition, other interventions often referred to as neurocognitive psychotherapies are proving quite effective for dealing with the day-to-day challenges that a student with AD/HD must face. Combining cognitive behavior therapy that focuses on the psychological issues of AD/HD (e.g., self-esteem, self-acceptance, self-blame) with the cognitive rehabilitation approach that focuses on life management skills (e.g., improving cognitive functions, learning compensatory strategies, and restructuring the environment), neurocognitive psychotherapy has been found to be extremely effective when treating students with AD/HD.

Are support groups helpful?

Support groups can be extremely helpful and, well, support-ive! Just make sure they are geared towards and composed of students with similar disabilities (AD/HD and/or LD). It is here that you will find other students who know exactly what you are going through. These groups can be very validating and empowering! Hearing the struggles and successes of other students with AD/HD can provide insight into your own difficulties and offer a model of how you can deal with similar situations. In addition, these students can be a wealth of information about what's available on campus and in the greater community and how you can handle various problems you encounter. One group that I worked with in Washington, DC even held an intervention for a student with AD/HD and LD who had developed a severe alcohol problem that was interfering with her life and safety.

A support group can be an informal get together of students with AD/HD or it can be organized and led by someone who has knowledge about and an interest in AD/HD from the disabilities or counseling office on campus. However, I feel so strongly about the benefit of support groups that I recommend if you can't find one on your campus . . . start one! They can be invaluable. I once worked with a group from a local university that met weekly to encourage each other and share information about various professors and courses. They ended up creating a booklet for all students with AD/HD on campus that rated professors and courses as AD/HD-friendly or not.

➡ **Extra, Extra!**

Here are some national organizations that may offer additional information and support:

Children and Adults with Attention Deficit/Hyperactivity Disorder (CHADD): http://www.chadd.org

Attention Deficit Disorder Association (ADDA): http://www.add.org

National Center for Girls and Women with AD/HD: http://www.ncgiadd.org

Learning Disabilities Association of America (LDA): http://www.ldanatl.org

Association on Higher Education and Disability (AHEAD): http://www.ahead.org

Chapter 6
Maintaining a Healthy Lifestyle

How do I go about designing a plan for healthy living?

Let's look at what a plan for healthy living would consist of—first, physical health (such as eating right, taking care of yourself, exercising, and getting enough sleep) and second, mental health (such as stress reduction, exercise, medications, dealing with coexisting conditions and past traumas). Designing a plan for healthy living means setting goals in these areas, being accountable to yourself (and, even better, someone else), along with improving the skills you'll need to help you reach these goals, In addition, you'll need to balance the time you need to meet class obligations, and the time you need to relax and be with friends. These topics are all covered in more detail in the answers to the next several questions.

I have trouble waking up in the morning; what can I do to get to class on time?

The first thing I would suggest is to look at the cause(s) of why you can't get up. Most likely it is because you didn't go to bed at a reasonable hour the night before, are not getting enough sleep, and, therefore, having difficulty waking up the next morning. Or perhaps it is a case of alarm clocks not working for you in high school, so you relied on your parents to act as human alarm clocks, waking you up each morning. If you are a deep sleeper or if you have only fallen asleep a few hours before you need to get up, you may not even hear the loudest alarm. If your parents were part of the equation in high school and you haven't yet learned how to fall asleep and wake up independently at college, you run the risk of missing classes or even sleeping through exams, which can affect your grades.

Here are some tips to help you create a plan to wake up and get to class on time in the morning. But, more importantly, it will help you to get adequate sleep. If you're rested you'll feel better the next day.

Analyze the reasons you have trouble waking up. Take a minute and try to determine the reasons that you might have difficulty waking up in the morning. Is it because you haven't gotten to sleep at a reasonable hour and are still tired? Are you just not a morning person? Does it take you a long time to wake up even on the weekends? Would taking classes later in the day be better? Do you sleep through the alarm? Or push snooze too often?

Find out what works. Would it be better for you to prepare what you'll need for classes the night before when you are more alert? Would meeting up with a friend help you get started? Try to identify the times when it has been easier for you to get yourself up. What motivated you then? Can you duplicate that scenario each morning?

Plan ahead. Think about what you can do the night before to make things go more smoothly in the morning. Selecting your clothes, thinking about what you'll have for breakfast, showering, gathering your books in one place, and checking your backpack are just a few ways that you might save minutes that will prevent you from being late once again.

Create a nighttime routine. Finding ways to get to sleep in the evening is important to ensure that you get enough sleep. Create a relaxing routine that will help you fall asleep. See the tips on pages 75–79 for ways to help you fall asleep more easily.

Find the ideal alarm. Explore ideas for alarms that will do the job of waking you up. Would a clock radio set on a loud station work better than an alarm? How about several alarms staggered to go off at different times or placed in different parts of the room? Check out extra-loud alarms or vibrating alarms that can be placed under your pillow. The latter might be helpful if you have a roommate. Does your phone or computer have an alarm? What about a rolling alarm that rolls off of furniture onto the floor and continues moving until you get out of bed to turn it off? And remember, there are call services that will call you in the morning (and I don't mean your parents!) for a monthly fee.

How can I get more sleep?

Getting to bed at a reasonable time and getting enough sleep is easier said than done. In general, life at college is at total odds with getting enough sleep. In the dorms there is always someone around to talk to or hang out with at any time of day or night. No one keeps track of lights out and you can always find food if you are hungry! If you have AD/HD the problem may be compounded by an actual sleep disorder Sleep disorders are very common in adults with AD/HD. A recent study (Surman, et al., 2009) found that adults with AD/HD went to bed later than control subjects and had a wider range of bedtimes, were more likely to take over an hour to fall asleep, and were more likely to experience difficulty getting to bed, going to sleep,

➥ Extra, Extra!

If you have trouble getting out of bed in the morning, explore different kinds of alarm clocks to see what works best for you. Here are some you could try:

Citrus Alarm Clock: http://www.ornj.net/citrus. This software alarm clock can set different alarms for different days, which is good for students with varied schedules. You can use your own mp3s as alarms.

Clocky: http://www.alarmclocksonline.com/clocky.htm. Clocky is a rolling alarm clock that rolls off furniture onto the floor and continues moving around until you get out of bed to turn it off.

Online Alarm Clock: http://onlineclock.net. This is a free web-based alarm clock that you can access on any computer.

SleepCycle: http://mdlabs.se/sleepcycle/index.html. This iPhone app monitors your movement while you sleep and wakes you while you are in your lightest sleep phase. It can also create graphs of your sleep cycles.

sleeping restfully, or waking in the morning. They also experienced more daytime sleepiness. Many teens and adults with AD/HD also get into the habit of being "night owls." They seem to become more alert as the day wears on and they prefer to work late at night when it is quiet and everyone else has gone to bed.

If you are having problems with any of these issues, don't panic. There is plenty that can be done. First of all, now that you are at college, you'll have the opportunity to schedule classes that best fit your patterns of alertness. If you really do your best work later in the day, try to schedule classes later in the day or evening. That will allow you to sleep in. Do yourself a favor and don't schedule any 8 a.m. classes if you know you won't be able to get there on time, or are likely to cut the class more often than you'll make it there. You most likely will not be at your best in these classes even if you make it to class.

Even if you can sleep until noon every day, it's best to try to get to bed at a reasonable hour. Remember, you won't always be able to schedule all of your classes later in the day and you might find that you need more time during the day to get your work done.

➡ **Extra, Extra!**

For more information on the importance of sleep, check out:

"The Importance of Sleep in College" (video): http://www.youtube.com/watch?v=XXV-46Pd8C0

The National Sleep Foundation's 2011 "Sleep in America" poll: http://www.sleepfoundation.org/article/press-release/annual-sleep-america-poll-exploring-connections-communications-technology-use-

Your sleep patterns are not out of your control. Try one of the following tips; they might help.

Analyze the reasons why you aren't getting to sleep at a reasonable hour. Do you wait until too late to get started studying? Are you more inefficient at night? Would it be better to study earlier? Do you spend too much time gaming or on social media? Do you sit up talking late into the night? Would a date for lunch or dinner be a better time to talk?

Check out your caffeine intake. Many students with AD/HD are used to self-medicating with caffeinated beverages or pills to help them focus, stay awake, and be more alert. This excess caffeine intake, however, can make it difficult for you to fall asleep at night. It may also make you nervous and jittery, especially when combined with a prescription stimulant to treat your AD/HD. It's better for your health overall to decaffeinate yourself and get the proper diagnosis and treatment for your AD/HD.

Look at your AD/HD medication schedule. Are you taking your medication as prescribed? Are you taking it so late in the day or evening that it is keeping you from falling asleep? Insomnia is a common side effect of most medications used to treat AD/HD. (See page 94 for a discussing of medication side effects.) If you find that it is difficult for you to fall asleep on days you take your medication, discuss this with your prescribing physician. A reduced dose, a dosage schedule change, or switching to another medication may help you get more sleep.

Check out your individual sleep needs. When you are trying to set up a sleep schedule, it's important to determine how much sleep you actually require. You might ask your parents how much you slept when you were younger and didn't have so much work to do. How many hours would you naturally sleep while on vacation, if you didn't have to get up to go somewhere? How many hours would you like to sleep? By looking at the answers to these questions, you may be able to estimate how much sleep you should be aiming for now. Listen to your body. After a good night's sleep you should feel rested and invigorated. Do you? If not, maybe something else is going on (e.g., sleep apnea or restless leg syndrome). Check it out with a professional.

Determine a time for lights out and set a reminder alarm. Students with AD/HD often have difficulty with transitions. Stopping what you are doing and getting ready for sleep may be extremely difficult. Once you've determined how much sleep you need, select a time for lights out and write it on your master schedule. If you need help with shutting down, set an alarm to remind yourself.

Set up a nighttime routine. This can really help you settle down and rid yourself of worry and uncertainty that affect sleep. Habits and routine make it less likely that you will forget important medications or duties.

Try progressive muscle relaxation. A great technique for relaxing and getting to sleep, progressive muscle relaxation is described in this guide on pages 60–61.

Try sleep relaxation tapes or brain wave training. These are described in more depth on pages 61–62.

Try deep breathing. Deep breathing exercises are known to be effective for relieving stress and anxiety. (See pages 58–59 for a more in-depth discussion of this technique.) You could also try using the NightWave, a relaxation device that makes use of deep breathing. The NightWave emits a soft blue light. The luminance of the light slowly rises and falls. You learn to synchronize your breathing with the rise and fall of the light. The light shuts off automatically after a time. You may fall asleep before that happens. Focusing on the light allows you to escape the buzzing thoughts commonly described by those with AD/HD as the reason they have difficulty falling asleep. If you have this problem, you might try this device. It can also be used if you wake up in the middle of the night, as it can be reset to get back to sleep.

Get enough exercise during the day.   This is really important, particularly if you are hyperactive, restless, or just have excess energy. Getting exercise each day has been shown to decrease hyperactivity.

Take a hot shower.   Not only will this help you relax at bedtime, but for those of you who like to sleep a little later, it will have the added benefit of giving you more time in the morning.

Plan for the next day.   This includes checking your schedule for the next day, deciding what you'll wear, and gathering up any necessary materials, books, or projects so you won't have to spend time looking for them in the morning.

Check it out.   If you still are having serious problems with falling or staying asleep, maybe you need a sleep study. Visit your university health clinic and discuss the problems you are having with a physician. Most communities now have hospitals or clinics that have sleep study centers, so you should be able to get a referral for a study locally.

Talk to your doctor about medications.   Until you know what is going on and have spoken to a professional, avoid the use of sleep aids, melatonin, and antihistamines plus pain medication such as Tylenol PM or Advil. Speak with your prescribing physician about the use of medications to help you sleep and how they should be taken with your stimulant medication. If necessary, your health care professional can prescribe something for you.

How can I eat right and choose healthy foods if I'm on a meal plan or if I can't cook?

At college you are totally in charge of what you eat and when. As a result, many college students, especially those with an unlimited meal plan, can go overboard and eat more than they normally would. In addition to cafeteria food, most campuses now have food courts with easy access to many of the more popular fast food chains. If you have not had experience with planning meals or making good food choices in the past, the temptation to eat these fast foods, because they are convenient and taste good, can be overwhelming. Access to take-out late into the night can also sabotage any semblance of a healthy diet.

Other students with AD/HD often find that they don't eat well for different reasons. Some college students report that other responsibilities are continually getting in the way of eating or that they get distracted and simply forget to eat on schedule. Time management problems cause them to grab food while on the go, often not making the best choices. Others don't make time for meals when their lives become too stress-filled. Some students who take medication for their AD/HD find that it suppresses their appetite during the day. These same students then tend to binge late at night when the medication wears off and they become hungry. So, how can you deal with these issues and begin to eat a balanced and healthy diet? Trying all or some of the following strategies may help you develop a plan.

Learn to make healthy choices.   Limiting fat intake, decreasing the amount of fried foods and sweets you eat each day, and increasing the number of fruits and vegetables can be a place to start. To go a little further you might consider switching to whole grains. Consult a nutritionist on campus or locally if you find you want more personalized information.

Find a role model.   Most colleges offer nutritional advice to student athletes. In addition to getting plenty of exercise, these student athletes usually make some pretty healthy choices when eating. Seek out these students in your dorm or fraternity/sorority and ask if they might give you some advice or eat with you when they are available.

Enlist a friend.   If you have problems with shopping, cooking, or preparing food for yourself, ask a roommate or another friend to teach you. They probably would love the help in the kitchen and your company while shopping.

Eat with others.   Eating is always more fun when you do it with others. Try eating with friends whenever you get the chance. By setting up a specific date and time, you'll be more likely to stop what you are doing and join them for a meal.

Take a class.   Most communities offer cooking classes at night or on the weekends. Get a group of friends together and sign up for one. You'll not only learn how to cook various dishes, but also get to eat what you prepare!

Get into a routine.   Try to get into the habit of eating regularly. Write it on your schedule and follow through. After a few weeks your body will expect to be fed on time and send out signals that it is hungry. Be sure to pay attention to this natural mechanism, stop what you are doing, and take a break for nourishing food. You'll feel better and have more energy.

Set small, specific goals. Maybe you need to gain or lose a few pounds, or try to eat more vegetables, or limit the amount of fast food or take-out you are consuming. Whatever the case, setting small, specific goals will help you accomplish this task. (See the discussion of SMART goals on pages 36–37.)

Reward yourself. Who doesn't like a treat? As part of your new goal of eating healthier, don't forget to include some treats as well. Pizza, pretzels, nuts, and other snacks can be part of a healthy diet, just not all the time or in place of meals!

Get help. If you find you are having more serious problems, such as bulimia, anorexia, or simply using food as a stress reliever, it's probably time to get help from the counseling center or campus psychiatrist.

I have AD/HD and I always seem to be bingeing or dieting. Could I have an eating disorder as well?

Your suspicions may indeed be well founded. Recent studies have documented a higher incidence of eating disorders in both adult women and adolescent girls with AD/HD, and established that impulsivity and the diagnosis of AD/HD-combined subtype were the best predictors of adolescent eating abnormalities (Surman, Randell & Biederman, 2006; Mikami, et al., 2008). Reports indicate that girls with AD/HD are 5.6 times more likely to develop bulimia and 2.7 times more likely to develop anorexia nervosa than girls without AD/HD (Biederman, et al., 2007).

The AD/HD–disordered eating connection is not difficult to understand. Eating disorders and AD/HD share several key characteristics, including impulsivity (lack of self-regulation), depression, and low self-esteem. However, women and girls with AD/HD develop eating disorders for many reasons. Symptoms of AD/HD can contribute to the development of binge eating and other disordered eating patterns as a woman loses her ability to control what she eats and how she responds to events in her environment. Many women with AD/HD eat for stimulation or to feel better. Others get distracted, forget to eat, and then have no control once they impulsively start eating. These eating patterns often result in chronic overeating and obesity, as these women have no idea how many calories they are consuming each day.

Treatment for many of these disordered eating patterns may best be accomplished by treating the AD/HD symptoms that underlie them. An eating disorder specialist described six patients with bulimia and AD/HD who were treated with dextro-amphetamine (Dukarm, 2005). All six patients reported no further episodes of binge eating and purging following treatment. These cases, along with recent clinical study findings, seem to confirm the association between bulimia and binge eating and AD/HD in girls and women, and have important clinical and treatment implications. In 2006, Dr. Dukarm presented a more detailed look at the potential role of AD/HD in the treatment of women with bulimia. If you feel that your eating has become a problem, contact your health care professional or someone in the counseling center to discuss your concerns.

⮕ **Extra, Extra!**

You can read more about AD/HD and eating disorders (ED) in:

Dukarm, C. *Pieces of a puzzle: The link between eating disorders and ADD*. Washington, DC: Advantage Books.

How do I fit exercise into my schedule with everything else I have to do?

Most people think that they need to join a gym, use fancy exercise equipment, or work out in a 60-minute aerobics class in order to get sufficient exercise. Well that doesn't need to be the case. The struggle is how to motivate yourself to exercise *regularly*. Most people with AD/HD are turned off by boring or unstimulating exercise routines. Over the years, I have found that two important rules can help here—variety and brevity. Keep it short and sweet, and add variety and spontaneity! As little as 20–30 minutes a day of physical exercise can provide substantial health benefits (both physical and mental). To motivate yourself, try the following tricks:

Join or create a group.   Get a group of friends together and schedule a time to meet for a walk, run, or pick-up game; sign up for dance, yoga, or aerobics classes; or join a team (such as rowing, soccer, basketball, even bowling). The company and commitment will keep you coming back.

Get someone else involved.   Hire a trainer. Believe me, this will keep you motivated and on track. Once you see the results and hopefully get bitten by the exercise bug, you'll be ready to go it on your own.

If you must walk on a treadmill, try to keep it interesting. Listen to music or watch TV—anything to keep yourself motivated. You might even schedule your exercise around a favorite TV show; that way, you'll be less likely to miss the show (and exercise)!

Set a goal. It might be as simple as walking around the block without "huffing and puffing" or walking or running in a charity event.

Keep it simple and be creative. Ten minutes several times a day can add up. Try the old tricks of walking to your dorm instead of taking the campus bus or parking farther away from the entrance when you go to the mall.

Take the stairs. I once knew a cardiologist who exercised by walking up and down the stairs of his office building several times a day between patients. Who says you're too busy?

➥ Extra, Extra!

For extra motivation to reach your fitness goals, check out these sites:

Runkeeper: http://runkeeper.com. An online community-based fitness tracker, which includes smartphone apps.

MapMyRide: http://www.mapmyride.com. An online community with a focus on using GPS tools to log runs, bike rides, hikes, and swims.

Chapter 7
Understanding Your Medication

What should I know about the medication I take for AD/HD?

First, you should know the name of your medication, why you are taking it (your symptoms), how it works, how long each dose lasts, and its most common side effects. Over the years, I have met many students who are unfamiliar with one or all of these aspects of their medication. In order to decide whether you need to continue or switch your medication, change the amount, or alter your dosing schedule while at college, you will need this information. In the past, the choice of taking medication or not was very likely not up to you. Hopefully, you have thought about your AD/HD, how it affects you and decided to continue taking medication at college, because you have seen the benefits and feel you need to continue to address these issues.

Stimulants are the treatment of choice for AD/HD and have been found to be highly effective, but they need to be taken consistently. Stimulants have been shown to improve cognitive functioning, but you'll need to work on syncing your medications and your study schedule to get the most from them. Taking medication before classes enhances information processing and can help you concentrate on what is being presented. Time spent studying will also be more effective if you are on your medication. It is therefore critical that you proactively discuss your needs with your prescribing physician and together decide what type of medication and dosing schedule will best meet your needs. Once you determine how long your medication is effective, you can set up a schedule for classes and study time accordingly. In addition, stimulants have been shown to improve reading comprehension. Students frequently report that, off medication, they find that they have read all of the material but don't have a clue as to what they have just read because they weren't paying attention. To avoid this problem, be sure that your stimulant medication is still in effect when you are reading.

AD/HD is a chronic, life-long disorder, and if you needed stimulant medication to concentrate in high school, you will most likely need the same or similar medication to do well in college. However, some college students decide when they enter college that they want to try to go off of their medications or just take them as needed for classes, studying for exams, or writing papers. The decision to go off meds should not be made without a great deal of thought and discussion with lots of people. A big transition like going to college might not be the best time to make such a change. You also need to keep in mind that they may not be as effective if you only take them sporadically.

This same advice also applies for medications that you might be taking for your depression or anxiety, conditions commonly seen in students with AD/HD. Often, because these medications are working as they should, you might feel better and mistakenly decide that you no longer need them. Going off these medications may have significant negative consequences (an increase in depression or suicidal thoughts) and should not be undertaken lightly. Before stopping any of these medications please discuss these possibilities with your therapist or healthcare physician.

What medications are available to treat AD/HD?

Stimulants are the most commonly prescribed medications for treating the symptoms of AD/HD. There are two classes of stimulants, those containing methylphenidate (Ritalin, Focalin, Concerta, Metadate, and Daytrana) and those containing amphetamines (Dexadrine, Adderall, and Vyvanse). Stimulants may be short-acting (usually lasting 4-6 hours) or long-acting (9-12 hours) depending on the formulation. Keep in mind that effectiveness is often not seen for 30 minutes for the short-acting products to 1–2 hours for the longer-acting products. In addition to the stimulants, there are a few non-stimulants now being used alone or in combination with the stimulants to treat the symptoms of AD/HD. These non-stimulants include atomoxetine (Strattera), guanfacine (Intuniv), and clonidine (Kapvay).

I have listed the various medications used to treat AD/HD and what we know about them in Table 7-1 following this section. Take a few minutes now to find out more about your medication.

How do medications used to treat AD/HD work?

All of these medications reduce the symptoms of AD/HD by targeting what is going on with the chemical neurotransmitters in your brain. These medications enhance brain functioning by inhibiting the breakdown of certain neurotransmitters (dopamine and norepinephrine), enhancing neurotransmitter receptor sensitivity, and acting as a neurotransmitter themselves. These actions allow signals to be transmitted across the synapse (space) between the brain cells (neurons), thus improving the efficiency of the various neuronal networks responsible

Table 7-1. Medications Used to Treat AD/HD Symptoms

Stimulants

Containing Methylphenidate

Shorter-acting Duration 3-4 hours	Dosages available	Website
Ritalin	5mg; 10mg; 20mg	n/a
Focalin™	2.5mg; 5mg; 10 mg	n/a
Methylin	5mg; 10mg; 20 mg	n/a
Longer-acting Duration 8-12 hours	**Dosages available**	**Website**
Ritalin SR	20mg	n/a
Ritalin® LA	10mg; 20mg; 30mg; 40mg	n/a
Metadate® CD	10mg; 20mg; 30mg; 40mg; 50mg; 60mg	http://www.metadatecd .com
Concerta®	18mg; 27mg; 36mg; 54mg	http://www.concerta.net
Focalin XR	5mg; 10mg; 15mg; 20mg	http://www.focalinxr.com
Methylin ER	10mg; 20mg	n/a
Daytrana Patch	10mg; 15mg; 20mg; 30mg	http://www.daytrana.com

Containing Amphetamines

Shorter-acting Duration 4-5 hours	Dosages available	Website
Dexedrine (dextroamphetamine)	5mg; 10mg	n/a
Adderall (mixed amphetamine salts)	5mg;7.5mg; 10mg; 12.5mg; 15mg;20mg;30mg	n/a

Longer-acting Duration 8-14 hours	Dosages available	Website
Adderall XR™ (mixed amphetamine salts mimics twice a day dose)	5mg; 10mg; 15mg; 20mg; 25mg; 30mg	http://www.adderallxr.com
Dexedrine Spansule (dextroamphetamine)	5mg; 10mg; 15mg	n/a
Vyvanse (lisdexam-fetamine, a prodrug activated in the body)	20mg; 30mg; 40mg; 50mg; 60mg; 70mg	http://www.vyvanse.com

Non-Stimulants

Longer-acting Duration 24 hours	Dosages available	Website
Strattera (atomoxetine)	10mg; 18mg; 25mg; 40mg; 60mg; 80mg; 100mg	http://www.strattera.com
Intuniv* (guanfacine)	1mg; 2mg; 3mg; 4mg	http://www.intuniv.com
Kapvay (clonidine, extended release)	0.1mg	http://www.kapvay.com

* now approved for use with stimulants to enhance treatment of AD/HD

for attention and executive functioning. (See pages 20–22 for a discussion of executive functioning.) Studies have shown that for some individuals with AD/HD, the problem may not be an actual lack of the neurotransmitter dopamine, but an excess of dopamine transporter protein, which carries the dopamine from the synapse back in to the cell where it is broken down, creating a relative lack of the dopamine. The stimulant methylphenidate has been shown to block dopamine transporter protein, resulting in an increase in available dopamine. Other stimulants and non-stimulants work on these same neurotransmitters to normalize functioning, all in slightly different ways. The important point, however, is that these medications are all working specifically on the biochemical abnormalities associated with AD/HD to allow for symptom and behavior control by improving functioning in specific areas of the brain.

Where do I go for my prescriptions on campus and who should I be checking in with about my medication?

Now that you are at college, it's important that you check in with the Disabled Student Services (DSS) office with your documentation so that they can certify that you are a student with special needs. Once that is done, you can then get in contact with the university health center to make an appointment with a physician who can continue to write prescriptions for your monthly medication refills while you are enrolled at the college. I do not recommend that you continue to call home to get a prescription and have your parents fill and mail it to you at school. You need to be responsible for your medications and have direct and immediate access to someone on campus that you can contact to discuss changes in your needs or any side effects you may experience. If your college does not have anyone that can prescribe medications for you, ask for a referral to a local psychiatrist or primary care physician who consults with the college on such matters. A letter from your initial prescribing physician may also be helpful in informing campus or local physicians about your symptoms, diagnosis, and previous medication and prescribing history. You should continue to see your primary prescribing physician back home at least once a year for re-evaluation as he or she probably knows you better.

How do I know if my medication is working?

Check-ins with a professional are important—but it's easy to determine if your medication is working if you know what to look for. Keep in mind that for your medication to work, you need to take it as prescribed. Be sure to take your medication every day at the time and dose prescribed. If you have difficulty remembering to take a dose, work with your physician or AD/HD coach to develop an effective reminder system such as setting a watch alarm or establishing a link between taking a pill and an external cue. If remembering multiple doses throughout the day is problematic, ask your physician if one of the newer once-daily formulations or the Daytrana patch would be a better option for you.

Once you are sure that you are consistently taking your medication, it's time to assess its efficacy. As part of the evaluation you underwent to diagnose you with AD/HD, your physician most likely asked you and possibly others to complete various rating scales that looked at symptoms and everyday functioning. In addition, you may have set target symptoms to guide the effectiveness of the treatment program. Both of these (rating scales and target symptoms) can help you determine if your medication is at the ideal dose to provide an optimum response.

The main goals of treating AD/HD are to reduce symptoms and normalize functioning. Instead of subjectively rating improvement, you and your physician can monitor your progress and determine when these goals are achieved by observing when your symptoms, as documented on rating scales, fall to within the range of scores seen in individuals without AD/HD. Ratings can be made weekly and guide increases in dose to an optimum response. If target symptoms do not respond to increasing doses of a particular medication, you'll know that medication is not working and another medication may be tried.

What is the best medication to treat AD/HD?

There is no such thing as the "best" medication to treat AD/HD. Every person with AD/HD has a unique set of symptoms and a specific response to medication. In general, the best medication to treat AD/HD is the one on which a person functions at his or her best with minimal side effects. That being said, how can you find this balance? Your physician will do this by working with you to find the medication and dose that best control your symptoms. Usually physicians start the dose of medication at the lowest recommended level and then increase the dose in small increments every week or so while continuously monitoring its effects and inquiring about side effects. Higher doses are more likely to provide optimal results, but may also produce more side effects. Side effects may occur at any dose level and are usually mild to moderate and diminish over time. (See page 94 for a discussion of side effects.) The dose of medication you end up on with stimulants is not determined based on weight or age, but rather by your individual needs and response.

Working closely with your physician *before* you get to college will allow you to get the best response from your treatment. Once the medication and dose has been established, however, it's important to take your medication as prescribed. Don't self-medicate! Because a certain dose works well, that doesn't mean that more medication will work better. Over the years I have worked with students who thought it was okay to increase their medication on their own during exam times or to complete a big project or paper, only to find out that things got worse for them. Please don't make that mistake!

Should I take medication on weekends and over breaks?

AD/HD affects all aspects of your life, not just academics. Think about it. You don't need to pay attention only in class. You also need to focus on what your friends are saying or on instructions on the job. Concentration is important in sports, whether you are playing tennis, throwing a baseball, or on the back nine in golf. Often, being distracted or acting impulsively can get you in trouble with your friends, or worse, when driving, with the law. It is important that you take some time now and assess whether your AD/HD is affecting your functioning or relationships and plan to take your medication accordingly. If you are not sure, try taking your medication for a few days to see the results. Be courageous and ask your friends for feedback. Improved attention may improve the quality of your life in many ways. I once worked with a girl who only took her medication on days she had classes. She was always complaining that she would have fights with her boyfriend on the weekends. At my suggestion, she tried taking her medication on the weekend as well and found that it significantly improved her relationship with her boyfriend. No more fighting! They got along so much better, even he was amazed!

AD/HD symptoms can also impact your driving abilities. Studies have shown that AD/HD affects driving skills in teens and adults (Barkley, et al, 1996; Jerome, et al, 2006). In addition, some states are now passing distracted driver laws aimed at cell phone and CD use, but which could also possibly be applied to a driver with AD/HD who is not taking medication to address his or her inattention and distractibility. Acting responsibility may mean taking your medication whenever you are driving, but especially if you drive long distances to and from campus.

How do I deal with medication side effects?

It is important that you promptly report any side effects you experience to your prescribing physician either at home or on campus. Do not decide to stop your medication on your own. Instead, talk with someone about addressing any side effects. If your stimulant medication is effective and making a significant difference for you, there is no reason to stop taking it for mild or unpleasant side effects. If, however, you experience a serious side effect such as chest pain, palpitations, seizures, hallucinations, or an allergic reaction, seek medical attention immediately and do not take another dose of your medication until you are evaluated. The most common side effects of stimulants—appetite decrease, dizziness, insomnia, stomachache or nausea—can usually be dealt with by making a few simple changes. Your physician may decide to reduce the dose, alter the time you take your medication, or switch to another medication altogether.

When should I take my medication to get the most out of studying?

Medications to treat AD/HD work most effectively if taken regularly and at the same time each day. I often recommend that students take their medication every day to keep symptoms under control. Remember, AD/HD affects *all* aspects of your life, not just academics. That being said, let me take time now to answer your questions about studying. Once you have established the correct dose of medication to reduce symptoms of inattention and distractibility, and improve your focus and ability to concentrate, it's important to set up a study schedule for when your medication is most effective. If you are unsure when this is, check with your prescribing physician. Most medications that treat AD/HD take at least 30 minutes to an hour to begin working, and can peak at 3 to 6 hours. If you take your medication in the morning for classes during day, it most likely has worn off by early evening. If you tend to study later in the evening, it may be necessary for you to take another dose of long-acting medication in the afternoon or a short-acting medication in the evening. Make sure you let your prescribing physician know the times that you primarily spend studying. Many students have reported that once they got on the proper medication schedule, they were more efficient and productive in the evenings and were able to get their work done earlier, with fewer errors, better grades, and fewer late nights. It is also important to note that you should not take it upon yourself to decide to increase the dose of your medication to improve results of studying. (I have worked with students who attempted this during exams with disastrous results.) Be aware that just because a certain dose of stimulant works well, that does not mean that more will work better. In fact, just the opposite may be true. I definitely urge you to work with your physician to regulate dosage, and caution against self-medicating.

⤷ **Extra, Extra!**

Here are a couple tools you could use to help you keep track of your medication:

Watchminder: http://www.watchminder.com. You can program this wristwatch to vibrate at certain times, to discreetly remind you to take your medication.

RxmindMe: http://www.rxmind.me. This free iPhone app helps you remember and track your prescriptions.

Can I drink coffee, tea, and other caffeinated drinks if I take medication for AD/HD?

The answer to this question has two parts. First, it's important to be careful with the amount of caffeine that you consume until you know how it interacts with your medication; and second, using caffeine to self-medicate, stay awake, or for extra energy is definitely a bad idea. I think it's important to make a distinction between these two!

While it is difficult for some people to stop all caffeine intake altogether, it's important to look at your total daily consumption, particularly if you are taking stimulants for your AD/HD. Most of the medications used to treat AD/HD are stimulants. Caffeine is also a stimulant. Students with AD/HD are often used to taking in large quantities of caffeine as a way to stay alert and awake. It can even become a form of self-medication and, for some students, it might have been the only way of dealing with the symptoms of AD/HD before their diagnosis. When these students begin taking stimulants to treat their AD/HD this habit can become a problem. If they do not reduce their caffeine intake, many complain that they are nervous and jittery, and have problems sleeping. These students often blame the medication for these side effects when in reality it is the large quantities of caffeine that they are consuming. So, when taking medicine for AD/HD, try to cut back on the caffeine, if not cut it out altogether, to avoid these unpleasant side effects.

What about drinking alcohol or taking drugs while on AD/HD medications?

On most college campuses today, it's a well-known fact that drinking, in particular, and drugs, to a lesser extent, can be hard to avoid. It is also a fact that most medications to treat AD/HD do not mix with drugs or alcohol. For many students with AD/HD this can present a great dilemma.

AD/HD is caused by a chemical imbalance in the brain. Stimulant medications work to correct this imbalance. (See page 87 for an explanation of how stimulants work.) If you use other drugs, such as marijuana, which affects brain dopamine, you can wreak havoc with an already imbalanced system. Medications to treat AD/HD may not be as effective, and functioning may become more impaired. Taking stimulants may also affect the metabolism of alcohol. Mixing the two can result in higher blood alcohol levels and increase the risk of alcohol poisoning. Mixing cocaine and stimulant medications can kill!

While the best thing to do when on any medication is to avoid these substances, it might not be realistic or comfortable to completely abstain on a college campus—although you can usually find support in the form of chemical-free housing for students who do want to completely avoid alcohol and drugs. Drinking in moderation is wise for everyone, but it is especially important for those with AD/HD. I would suggest that if you must drink while taking your medication that you only have one drink. If you feel that's impossible, skip your medication in the afternoon when you are drinking at night, or skip your medication in the morning if you are drinking earlier in the day and are on a long-acting medication on weekends.

However, remember that if you skip medication, you may become hyperactive, inattentive, or impulsive, and act inappropriately or engage in risky behaviors. Ask a trusted friend or significant other to keep an eye on you and to drive you home. I once had a patient who did not take his medication before going out drinking. When his behaviors became really out of control, he took his medication, resulting in his having to be admitted to a local emergency room. Please be careful and act responsibly. If you feel you are having a problem with drugs or alcohol, get help. There are many resources on campus to help with these issues. (See page 65 for more information on this topic.)

Can I get in trouble if I share my medication with my friends?

First, you should know that while possession of a controlled substance without a prescription is serious, distribution carries even stronger penalties. The simple answer to your questions is, "Yes, you could be arrested if you share or sell your medication." And it has happened to students with AD/HD. Stimulant medications have been classified by the Drug Enforcement Administration (DEA) and the Food and Drug Administration (FDA) as Schedule II Controlled Substances. This classification puts stringent restrictions upon how these drugs are prescribed and handled. It is against the law for you to distribute or sell a controlled substance. This means sharing your medication under any circumstances is against the law, even if it was for free. A gift is considered a sale in the eyes of the law. Giving a controlled substance to someone who does not have a legal or medical reason to possess it is the same as selling it. Besides, giving any medication to your friends is not only illegal, it may cause them harm if they are not being supervised by a doctor.

Second, the law mandates that all medications for the treatment of AD/HD be kept in their original container and labeled with your name and the name and dose of medication. It is important that you not transfer your stimulant medication to another bottle or carry it loose for any reason. In addition, to prevent theft, I recommend that all of my patients carry their medications with them at all times (usually in their backpacks) and avoid leaving them in their rooms where they may be more accessible to others.

If your friends find out that you have AD/HD and are taking stimulants, they may ask you to give or sell them some pills. While the opportunity to make a little money may be tempting, it's important that you set your priorities and put yourself first. You'll need your medication to perform your best and if you share or sell your pills, you'll have fewer for yourself.

How you deal with the pressure from others around this issue is important. It's important to realize that it might happen and to be ready. Make a plan and rehearse what you will say. Remember, if they really are your friends, they won't ask you more than a few times and will respect you when you stand up for yourself. If not, they really are not your friends, are they?

Lastly, several colleges have recently been dealing with the problem of students using "performance enhancing drugs" like stimulants to study, take exams, and write papers by making their use an honor code violation. As a result, both the student who used the non-prescribed medications and the student who supplied them may face automatic expulsion.

How do I handle the attitudes of others about having AD/HD and taking medication or getting accommodations?

Many students who don't have AD/HD feel that you have an advantage by receiving accommodations and that they, too, would do better academically if they could have more time on tests or take medication to improve attention, concentration, and focus. But they usually have no idea what having AD/HD is like, or how you may have suffered over the years. Rather than feeling badly when they question your reasons, it's important for both you and them that you take the time now to explain what having AD/HD is like. When you describe your symptoms and explain that AD/HD is similar to having allergies or diabetes in that they are all disorders that cannot be cured but can be controlled with medication and avoiding certain situations or foods, most people understand. Mention that these treatments only level the playing field, and do not give you an advantage. Your accommodations are like glasses and your AD/HD is like having poor vision: without glasses you can see, but not very well, and simply trying harder to see (or pay attention on a test) will not make it better. Staying later to complete a test, going to talk with your professors, asking for extensions, or finding someone to take notes for you only take more of your time, not less, and make your life more complicated. But all these things are necessary if you want to succeed. Most people with AD/HD would rather not have to bother with all of these accommodations (and some don't), but without them you would not do as well. Hopefully, this will help others understand a little better what having AD/HD is like.

In the end, however, you'll need to be careful about who you tell about your AD/HD. Not all people will be receptive and some will feel that you are just making excuses. You won't be able to convince everyone about AD/HD. Ultimately, you can choose not to associate with those who don't want to understand you better.

I have decided not to take medication for my AD/HD. Is there anything else that I can do to improve my symptoms?

First, make sure that you are getting plenty of exercise. There has been a lot of research showing that exercise definitely decreases hyperactivity and other symptoms of AD/HD (Ratey, 2008). Second, more and more people are becoming interested in alternative therapies and asking questions about them. Increasingly, individuals and experts alike are speaking about the value of meditation and yoga to train attention and regulate emotions. Mindfulness meditation training in adults and adolescents with AD/HD has been shown in some studies to decrease AD/HD symptoms in as many as 78 percent of participants (Zylowska, et al., 2008). I'll briefly discuss each one of these therapies below, but if you are interested and want further information, you might check with the counseling center on campus to see if they offer these services or know where you can find them.

Practice mindfulness meditation. This involves three basic steps: 1) bringing attention to an "attentional anchor" such as breathing; 2) noting that distraction occurs and letting go of the distraction; and 3) refocusing back to the "attentional anchor." This sequence is repeated many times during the course of each meditative session. As the individual becomes better able to maintain focus on the attentional anchor, the notion of "paying attention to attention" is introduced and individuals are encouraged to bring their attention to the present moment frequently during the course of the day. By directing one's attention to the process of paying attention, to noticing when one becomes distracted and refocusing attention when distraction occurs, mindfulness meditation training can be thought of as an "attention training" program.

Try yoga. You probably have heard of or even tried yoga before as a form of exercise, but may not have known it can help with AD/HD. Yoga combines physical movement and postures, breathing control, concentration, and relaxation to help you feel more in control. Research now supports the use of regular yoga in children with AD/HD. One study showed that yoga improves attention and behavior in school-age boys that were already stabilized on medication, compared to boys on medication only. Furthermore, the boys who practiced yoga more frequently had even better outcomes (Jensen & Kenny, 2004). Another study randomly selected children with AD/HD to practice either yoga or traditional exercise. The children who performed yoga had improved attention and fewer AD/HD symptoms compared to the exercise group (Haffner et al, 2006).

Educate yourself about alternative treatments. Alternative treatments are usually defined as treatments other than medication and behavioral interventions (psychosocial intervention) that claim to treat the symptoms of AD/HD with an equal or more effective outcome. These alternative treatments typically include elimination diets, supplements, neurofeedback, and working memory training. I'll briefly address each one here.

Elimination diets. With elimination diets for AD/HD, certain foods are eliminated from the diet to reduce AD/HD symptoms. Over the past several decades, there has been much controversy about sugar, additives, food coloring, and preservatives and their relationship to AD/HD symptoms such as hyperactivity. At this time, there is no proof that a diet high in sugar actually causes AD/HD. Years ago, the Feingold Diet proposed the elimination of artificial colorings, flavorings, and preservatives in order to decrease hyperactivity. While many studies have disproved Feingold's theory, individual children who have tried the elimination diet have reported an improvement (Nigg, et al., 2012). In 2007, the UK's Food Standards Agency (FSA) suggested that certain artificial colors, when paired with sodium benzoate, may be linked to hyperactive behavior. Still other studies have suggested that pesticides may be linked to an increase in AD/HD diagnosis in children (Bouchard, et al, 2010). I think the takeaway from all of this is that it's best to eat a healthy diet with lots of fruits and vegetables (organic if possible) that doesn't contain a lot of preservatives and artificial ingredients. If you are so inclined, organic is probably better for you.

Fish oil supplements. There is some evidence that fish oil can help improve AD/HD symptoms. Fish oil contains omega-3 fatty acids. There are some findings that suggest that, in children with AD/HD, fish oil supplements may improve mental skills. For instance, it may help improve a child's ability to organize activities. In one study, a specific supplement of fish oil and evening primrose oil was used. Results showed that it decreased hyperactivity and inattentiveness, and improved clear thinking and overall behavior in children with AD/HD (Arnold, et al, 1994; Johnson, et al., 2009).

St. John's wort. St. John's wort is a common herbal supplement and has been recommended and used for many years to treat depression, anxiety, and sleep disorders. This herbal treatment is thought to affect various brain chemicals, including serotonin, dopamine, and norepinephrine. However, recent scientific studies do not support the use of St. John's wort to treat AD/HD. In fact, recent findings conclude that St. John's wort has no effect on the symptoms of AD/HD at all (Weber, et al., 2008).

Neurofeedback. Neurofeedback intervention is based on findings that people with AD/HD have a particular brain wave pattern that involves an excess of theta waves and less than expected beta waves. Neurofeedback treatment involves teaching the patient how to increase their arousal levels by changing this brainwave pattern. The patient's brain activity is monitored through electrodes hooked up to their head. When the brain waves reach a desired frequency, a signal informs the patient. Through training, the patient can ultimately learn how to increase arousal on his or her own. While there has been some promising research in this area, more research is needed to determine the efficacy of neurofeedback on AD/HD symptoms. Training can be both time-consuming (often requiring 30–40 sessions) and expensive (costing as much as $3,000). If you are interested in this type of treatment and have the time to pursue the training, contact a local neurologist or psychologist who is familiar with this type of treatment. The following are some tips to make sure the person you are considering is legitimate: 1) look for a clinician certified by the Biofeedback Certification International Alliance who is either a licensed professional specializing in psychological or medical disorders, or working with someone who is; 2) determine whether the practitioner is a good fit by meeting with him or her before agreeing to a treatment plan; and 3) verify that the practitioner is using up-to-date methods and equipment, since the field is changing rapidly. Ask what research backs up the practitioner's methodology and what kind of training he or she has had.

Working memory training. Working memory is the ability to hold information in one's mind for later use. This skill is important for recall of information on tests and other related tasks. As discussed previously on pages 20–21, individuals with AD/HD frequently have problems with working memory as well as other executive functions. A training program, Cogmed, has recently been developed that can be carried out at home with the support and supervision of a trained coach. Promising results for this training program have been published in peer reviewed journals and presented at national scientific meetings (Klingberg, et al, 2005).

⤷ **Extra, Extra!**

Cogmed can be found around the world. To find a practitioner in your area, check out: http://www.cogmed.com/category/cogmed-in-your-area.

Chapter 8
Accessing Specialized Services

What types of services and supports are available on campus for students with AD/HD?

Utilizing college resources allows students with AD/HD the opportunity to be successful. Taking advantage of these opportunities along with academic accommodations (see Chapter 9) will not only improve your academic performance, but also enhance your self-confidence. Remember, successful students use resources!

The following campus resources are often available to all students, but can be used in a special way to help you address your AD/HD. I have listed specific adaptations or services that you might consider requesting next to each one. Think about which resources would benefit you.

Advising system. Colleges usually provide every student with an advisor. However, some schools also offer specialized academic advising through the Disabled Student Services (DSS) office for students with AD/HD. Finding an advisor knowledgeable about AD/HD is extremely important. If a student with AD/HD is sent, along with all other students, for academic advising by someone with little or no training in AD/HD, the advising is unlikely to be helpful. To assist students with AD/HD who have found themselves in this situation, I have often suggested that they look for faculty members who are knowledgeable about and sympathetic toward the needs of students with AD/HD. These faculty members can be found in various departments on campus and can often act as unofficial mentors providing significant help and support for the student with AD/HD. Advisors, once they ascertain your learning style, can advise you about course selections, help with a manageable (or reduced) course load, or provide access to early course registration.

Tutoring network. One-on-one or group tutoring is usually offered on most campuses. However, be sure to ask if specialized tutoring is available for students with AD/HD. Almost all campuses provide peer tutoring or teaching assistant (TA) help sessions; however, students with AD/HD typically need more specialized services from a trained tutor.

Special services librarians. In addition to providing a quiet place to study, many college libraries have special services librarians, who are available to assist you with research tools when you are conducting research for papers or projects. In most instances, you will first need to be qualified by the Disabled Student Services (DSS) office on campus to receive this assistance. Libraries also often offer specialized software and hardware to meet your needs, including voice-activated writing software.

Writing center. Be sure to inquire about the various types of writing supports available on campus for students with AD/HD. Many colleges offer programs that are different or more intensive than supports available to all students. Writing papers is often one of the greatest challenges for college students with AD/HD. Because of this particular set of challenges, it is most helpful if writing tutors are available who have specialized training and experience in working with students with AD/HD. Ask if they are available.

Counseling center. The counseling center usually provides psychological counseling for emotional as well as other mental health issues. This is the place to seek help with anxiety, depression, or stress. At some colleges where there is a psychiatrist on staff, medication management may be provided at the center. Drug and alcohol counseling, along with help for eating disorders, can also be found here on most campuses.

Health center. In addition to being available when you are sick, the health center may also have physicians available who can help you with your AD/HD challenges, as well as handle your medication needs, including refilling your medication prescriptions. This may also be an on-campus resource for mental health crises as well as drug and alcohol issues.

Fitness center. Here you'll find all kinds of programs and activities to meet your exercise needs. Often trainers are available to monitor or help you set up an exercise program. Most campus fitness centers are open late at night to accommodate your schedule.

Career counseling. As you near graduation, this resource may be an invaluable source of information as you begin your job search. Here you can find help with preparing a job search plan, writing your resume, or preparing for an interview. Inquire at the DSS office to see if they recommend a specific counselor for students with AD/HD. At some point you may also want to discuss with the career counselor whether or not you should disclose your AD/HD during your job search process. In most cases, I do not recommend disclosure routinely, but each case is different and the decision to disclose or not may be influenced by both the employer as well as the potential employee.

Should I join study groups?

Study groups can be very helpful, particularly if you are an auditory learner. (See pages 43–45 for a discussion of learning styles.) These groups will not only help you develop a more in-depth understanding of the material being covered, but also provide the structure and discipline to get you to focus on studying by making a commitment to meet with the group.

There are several levels to learning new material. Visual recognition is considered to be the lowest with the highest level being mastery or the ability to teach the material to others. When you participate in a study group, you are more likely to reach these higher levels. The various levels of learning are usually categorized as:

- Recognition: knowing material when it's presented to you
- Retrieval: being able to retrieve information without a cue or reminder
- Conceptual understanding: being able to explain the material to others
- Contextual understanding: putting material in context
- Mastery: being able to teach the material to others

Many students stop studying at the first level—after simply recognizing that they have seen the material before. Study groups can help you get to these other levels when learning new material. It is important, however, to choose your study group carefully. Asking the following questions may help you to decide if a group is right for you: Where will the group meet? A coffeehouse may be too distracting. A dorm room may be too crowded. When will they meet? If a group meets too late at night, your medications may have worn off, making it difficult for you to concentrate. Too early in the morning and you may not be alert. How many students will be in the group? Will a TA (teacher's assistant) be there to answer questions? If a group is too large, each member may not get to participate and you may not get your questions answered. Will the group have a social component? Some groups meet at mealtimes with each member bringing their food and eating during the meeting. Others order take-out with all members chipping in to pay the bill. Make sure the ground rules about this social aspect of the group are discussed ahead of time. Study groups can get side-tracked easily and become more focused on the social rather than the study aspect. Your time is important. Value it and make sure that you are spending it in a way that enhances your learning.

What other services and accommodations should I ask for?

Self-awareness is the key to selecting accommodations that will work for you and make the difference for success. Many students, however, are often not aware of either the accommodations that are available or the specific accommodations that will work for them. Based on your strengths and weaknesses and what has worked for you in the past, it is important to discern your needs and what accommodations might be useful based on those needs. The following list might help. Some students find it helpful to rate these accommodations as essential, good ideas, or optional, because it helps them to prioritize what to ask for.

- Special support program
- Study skills class (often offered to freshmen but upperclassmen may attend)
- Special advance registration
- Reduced course load
- Tutoring in specific subjects
- AD/HD coaching
- Quiet dorm
- Single dorm room
- Extended time on tests
- Note takers
- Help with writing papers
- Books on tape
- Advisor knowledgeable about AD/HD
- Library services and special services librarians
- Writing center
- Career counseling

Chapter 9
Obtaining Academic Accommodations

What are some of the specific academic accommodations available for students with AD/HD at college?

The following are some of the more common accommodations, modifications, and technology that college students with AD/HD have found useful. If you find that an accommodation sounds like it might be helpful to you, make a check in the box next to that accommodation. Remember, try to be specific and ascertain how this accommodation might help you based on your difficulties. Be selective! Every student doesn't need every accommodation. Some accommodations may actually be detrimental to your specific needs.

During lecture classes

☐ Sit near the front of the room.

☐ Use a note taker.

☐ Obtain copies of another student's notes.

☐ Use a smart pen for recording lectures (see page 116 for more information).

☐ Use a computer in all classes.

☐ Obtain copies of visual aids, PowerPoint presentations, or handouts to review before class.

☐ Obtain permission to leave for a brief break or stand in the back of the class every 30-45 minutes as necessary (for particularly long lectures).

☐ Take notes using a graphic organizer.

☐ Use the "close procedure" for note taking. Before the lecture, ask the teacher to give you a copy of the notes with blanks to fill in, or a list of key words.

During lab sessions

☐ Make sure you have an adequate workspace.

☐ Have a TA or someone else "man" your space while you take a break during long lab sessions.

☐ Review procedures for lab notebooks and any specific requirements with the instructor ahead of time.

In courses

☐ Obtain written instructions from professors.

☐ Reduce your course load.

☐ Do priority registration.

☐ Request a course substitution.

During examinations

☐ Get extended time for completion.

☐ Find a quiet, distraction-free environment.

☐ Alter the response format of a test.

☐ Alter the examination schedule.

☐ Take a longer examination over a period of time in shorter segments.

☐ Request take-home or open book exams.

☐ Obtain permission to record responses to questions on an examination. The professor would then grade these responses as an oral examination.

☐ Use formulas or other material during the test.

☐ Establish spelling and grammar requirements ahead of time.

For writing assignments

☐ Meet with the professor to clarify the writing assignment.

☐ Create a rubric to determine what the teacher expects the assignment to contain.

☐ Have rough drafts evaluated before handing in the final copy.

☐ Request extra time for completing assignments.

☐ Use an editor before submitting final drafts.

☐ Use a computer for in-class writing assignments.

☐ Use speech-to-text technology.

For reading assignments

☐ Use a reading program like Kurzweil to scan your book and read to you.

☐ Break up individual reading assignments into smaller sections.

☐ Use the syllabus to break up and schedule larger assignments over several days.

Auxiliary aids

☐ Request audio recordings of books and texts.

☐ Use a calculator or other device for tests and assignments.

☐ Employ organizers and schedules for tests and assignments.

⬆ Extra, Extra!

Be sure to check out the latest note-taking technology, like the Pulse Smart Pen: http://www.livescribe.com/. This relatively inexpensive pen (about $95) uses special notebook paper and synchronizes what is being said to the exact letter that was written at that point in the lecture. You don't have to worry about missing key details; you can go back later and tap the pen at the point on the page where you lost the lecture, and the pen will play back the words that were spoken at that time. With this pen and digital recorders, you can download the audio version of the lecture and make an audio file and listen to it over again. The pen allows you to download the actual written notes, listen to the audio over again, and modify the notes on the computer.

How do I get academic accommodations at college?

Accessing accommodations at college begins at the Disabled Student Services (DSS) office. But the catch is that you must self-disclose that you have a disability and request the services. No one is going to be looking for you and offering you these services. Unfortunately, only about 30 percent of students who received services for their AD/HD in high school access services in college (Newman, et al., 2009). We have already talked about this somewhat in the answer on page 27 to the question, "Are there any specific scenarios that make things worse at college for students with AD/HD?"

To qualify for services, you will need recent documentation of your disability. When you meet with the staff at the disabilities office, bring your documentation with you. Documentation must be up to date and you may need a new assessment to provide this required documentation if previous evaluations are too old. You will be required to pay for the evaluation.

The following information will be necessary when requesting accommodations from your college:

- Information and documentation showing your diagnosis of AD/HD, including any recent assessments;

- Types of academic accommodations that have worked for you in the past;

- Types of academic accommodations you anticipate needing in college;

- How AD/HD can contribute to your success in college; and

- How AD/HD affects your capacity to learn and study effectively.

In addition to setting up accommodations for you, the DSS office should also be able to refer to other resources on campus to address the specific needs that you thought helpful on page 112. While you may be able to get information about other services on campus, it's best to discuss them with someone who understands your needs. These advisors have been working with students on your particular campus for some time and have a good sense of what might work out best for you. Rather than struggling on your own or seeking help in the wrong place, set up a program that is likely to make a difference from the very start.

It's also extremely important that you have a sense of how your AD/HD affects you and what accommodations you think that you'll need to succeed. Here's where your needs assessment comes in.

You will have to repeat the process of requesting accommodations each semester, with new classes and new professors. It is important to stay on top of your needs and make sure you submit your request early, before classes start each semester.

I didn't have accommodations in high school; is that a problem?

In most instances that is not a problem, especially if you were recently diagnosed. However, at the college level, having a diagnosis alone won't qualify you for accommodations; your condition must impact you in some way. Colleges typically require recent documentation to demonstrate the impact of a disability, and each college can choose the guidelines they follow for the type of documentation they require. The laws governing college (Section 504 of the Rehabilitation Act and the ADA) give colleges the right to define their documentation guidelines. Most colleges won't accept an IEP (Individualized Educational Plan) or a 504 plan (document stating a student received accommodations in high school) anyway. Likewise, they will not accept a report from an outdated evaluation. To make matters even more confusing, there is no consistency in the documentation needed at the college level. What is needed at one college to be eligible for accommodations and services may be totally different from what is needed at another college—even within the same state! Therefore, you will want to check out the requirements for receiving services and accommodations at the Disabled Student Services (DSS) office on your campus. The earlier you begin gathering the documentation you need, the better. If you are a newly diagnosed student, contact the DSS office as soon as possible, but definitely before your next semester. If you are an incoming freshman who has previously been diagnosed or treated for AD/HD and feel you would likely require services at college, even though you didn't access them in high school, contact the DSS office as soon as you are accepted to that college or as soon as you make the decision that you will need services.

Who will tell my professors about my AD/HD?

In most instances the Disabled Student Services (DSS) office facilitates the communication of a student's disability needs to each professor. Disabled Student Services should provide official documentation of the student's disability and the accommodations for which he or she is eligible. In addition to asking how this is done (usually by letter), be sure to ascertain what types of supportive communication are provided for the student by the disability services in the event that a professor is not cooperative in providing accommodations. Does the DSS office help to mediate disputes between student and professor regarding rights and accommodations? Unfortunately, many college professors are still not aware of the legal rights of students with a documented disability such as AD/HD, and some are even hostile to the idea of providing accommodations to these students. The best way to maintain a positive relationship with professors, especially hostile ones, is to show them that you're engaged and ready to learn and work.

In most instances, it's important to have a good working relationship with your professors. Find out when their office hours are and go visit. As professionals, most professors want to help you succeed. Make sure you are both on the same page about obtaining and using accommodations in his or her class. It is your responsibility to follow the procedure to obtain alternative testing (extended time, use of a computer, or oral administration). Some schools require a complex set of steps each time a student with AD/HD requests alternative testing. While it may be difficult, if not impossible, for a student with organizational and time management problems to comply with such requirements, it is critical that you enlist the help of all involved to make sure that you receive all services you are entitled to.

Are requirements for graduation ever waived for students with AD/HD?

Colleges are not required by law to waive requirements for graduation. While your school can grant you a reduced course load each semester and waivers for specific math or foreign language requirements, the number of credits for graduation will usually not be reduced. Be sure to determine the school's policy toward course substitution when a student's disability prevents him from fulfilling a particular requirement toward graduation or his major area of study, such as a math or foreign language course, before attending that institution. The academic dean's office or your academic advisor can usually provide information on obtaining waivers or course substitutions for you.

I think I should qualify for a waiver for foreign language or math, but do I really have to try the course and fail first? Will this affect my GPA?

Sometimes, the college does require that a student attempt a course first, and that information is important to know as soon as possible. If in high school you had a great deal of difficulty with math or foreign language, it is critical that the flexibility of such requirements at a college be carefully considered before applying to that particular institution. Some schools that provide requirement waivers or course substitutions first require a student to take and fail the required course. If this failing grade becomes a permanent part of your undergraduate record, it can have a lasting negative effect upon your grade point average. So be careful, get the information, and choose your options wisely.

How can I learn to ask my professor for what I need?

Once you have determined your learning style (pages 43–45) and your strengths and weaknesses (pages 40–43), effective self-advocacy skills will be needed to activate the services and accommodations available to you. It's really important that you feel comfortable discussing your strengths and weaknesses and how your disability affects your learning. Being able to name and ask for the accommodations specifically is also critical. The following tips may help you accomplish this without being defensive.

First and foremost, it's important to take responsibility for your AD/HD and not use it as an excuse. Be ready to state that you want to complete the assignment or project but that your weakness in (list your areas of weakness) may get in the way of your doing the best possible job. Then be ready to engage in creative problem solving with your professor to determine ways to get the work done. Be sure to explain the difficulties you commonly have encountered in the past in advance of assignments or tests, rather than as an excuse after the fact. These difficulties may include going blank during a test or having difficulty putting your thoughts into writing or participating in class discussions. By forming a working relationship with your professor at the beginning of the semester, you'll be more likely to avoid negative outcomes. Don't wait until you are in trouble. Email or make an appointment to communicate and keep your professor up to date if you're having trouble with an assignment. Most professors will respect your self-knowledge and self-advocacy skills and value the fact that you want to do well, thus making them more willing to help.

How do I know when I need to make an appointment to talk with my professor or ask for help in a course?

To answer this question, assess the situation and look for any of the following signs that mean it's time to ask for help. First, it's important to inventory your feelings. Are you frustrated with a particular task or assignment? Or are you feeling stuck because you are working on the same problem or rereading the same material over and over and not getting anywhere? Are you unsure of the next step to take or which direction to go in to solve a problem? Are you confused or having difficulty understanding a concept being taught in class? Are you getting behind in your assignments and starting to feel stressed and panicky? If you answered "yes" to any of these questions, it might be time to ask for help. Consider making an appointment to meet with your professor or a counselor as soon as possible.

Do students with AD/HD get early registration privileges?

Early registration can be a very useful accommodation if you have AD/HD, as it allows you a better opportunity to hand-pick professors and customize your schedule based on your needs.

Your advisor should be able to get you this privilege, but you'll need to do a little advance legwork to take full advantage of it. Be sure that you are aware of your strengths and weaknesses (pages 40–43) and your learning style (pages 43–45) before choosing a particular class or section. You may also want to consult with your advisor or dean to ask for help balancing courses that require a great deal of reading with courses that require less reading. It is also important to balance lecture classes with more participatory classes, if possible. You might want to consider other prerequisites as well. These might include when a class meets (early morning versus later in the day or evening), the size of the class (large lecture versus smaller discussion class), the number of papers or exams that will make up the final grade, and any attendance requirements.

While this accommodation can be extremely useful, the greatest difficulty most students with AD/HD have is remembering to take advantage of it and to go online within the appropriate time frame to register for the classes they have chosen. If this might be a problem for you, work with your coach or a friend to set up a plan to remind you to act as soon as registration opens. You'll be glad you did!

Chapter 10
Hiring an AD/HD Coach

What is AD/HD coaching?

AD/HD coaching is a collaborative process that will help you make progress towards the realization of your goals. It uses the technique of questioning to assist you in finding your strengths and talents and taking action. AD/HD coaching can help you to better understand yourself and your disabilities, thus allowing you to become a better self-advocate. In addition, it provides the structure and accountability that you need in your life to function successfully in the college environment. Coaching operates on the premise that you have the answers to your problems and that by working with a coach you will be able to design a program that works best for you.

You are probably most familiar with the role that a coach plays in the world of athletics. Here a coach helps the individual gain new skills, develop a game plan, and press on despite any obstacles or difficulties encountered. Practice and hard work become the stepping stones to achieving the desired goal. When a student has AD/HD, accommodations at college may not be enough to allow him or her to succeed academically. Working with a coach may provide that student with the necessary structure and accountability to help him or her succeed.

Coaching is different from both tutoring and therapy. Coaching differs from tutoring in that it works on building executive functioning skills (such as time management and organization) and provides the structure and accountability necessary for success in life, not just academics. Tutoring often only works on content acquisition and improving skills in academic areas. Coaching is also different from therapy. Unlike therapy, where the professional brings a particular orientation and set of therapeutic skills to apply to a client's problem, the coach and coaching client mutually agree on what approach might work best for the particular client. A coach helps each client understand how AD/HD impacts his or her behaviors, gets involved in making changes in his or her life, and elicits creative strategies to serve the needs of each client.

How do I find a coach?

Finding a coach is not always easy. Some colleges now have coaches on staff in the Disabled Student Services (DSS) office to help students with disabilities. This office may also be able to refer you to someone on campus or in the community who provides coaching to students with AD/HD. AD/HD coaches are now available in more areas of the country, but remember that the coach does not need to be located where you are to establish a coaching relationship. Coaching can be done remotely over the phone or Skype with email or text check-ins.

There are also organizations that will provide coaches to college students, such as the EDGE Foundation (www.edge foundation.org) or the AD/HD Coaches Organization (ACO, www.AD/HDcoaches.org), which lists AD/HD coaches on their website.

An Internet search for AD/HD coaches will also give you more information about coaches in your area and direct you to their websites.

The important point is finding someone who is qualified, knowledgeable about AD/HD, and experienced in working with college students. You can have some sense of this by checking out the coach's website and then setting up a phone interview.

Here are some questions to ask when interviewing a potential coach:

- How long have you been involved in AD/HD coaching?
- How many clients do you have who are college students with AD/HD?
- How do you prefer to work (only face-to-face, by telephone, e-mail)?
- I have identified _____ as one of my needs. What is your experience in this area?
- How often do you anticipate we would need to meet?
- What are your fees? Per month? Per hour?
- Can you provide me with references (colleagues or former clients)?
- When would you be available to begin working together?

Once you have interviewed the coach and checked out any references, you should have a better sense of the coach as a person and whether or not you will be able to work with him or her.

How does coaching work?

Coaching is a partnership that supports the student in examining his or her strengths and weaknesses and developing the necessary strategies and interventions to deal with his or her AD/HD in a way that fosters success. Think of working with a coach as being part of a team. You and the coach will work together to identify problems and agree on strategies to overcome these difficulties. Coaches are usually flexible and can work with you in several different ways. This may include in person, by telephone, text, Skype, email, IM or an online webinar or other service. Face-to-face meetings may take place on campus or the coach's office or electronically. You may work with your coach alone, or at times include others as part of the meeting as needed. These others may include your counselor, physician, or professor.

Coaches may offer suggestions and reminders, and provide structure and boundaries, but they are not a parent, counselor, or friend. The coaching relationship helps you design the environment to meet your needs and become accountable for taking action. Despite the emphasis on grades and achievement, college is not just about academics. When a student has AD/HD, coaching usually focuses on improving time management and organization skills. AD/HD symptoms can, however, impact other areas. So, in addition to working on particular academic skill areas, the AD/HD coach may also support you in looking at lifestyle issues and setting goals to make the desired changes to create balance and promote success in all areas of your life. Areas such as diet, sleep habits, exercise, and other aspects of self-care may be examined in an effort to foster health and balance in your daily life so that you can achieve your goals and dreams.

How long does coaching usually last and what does it cost?

Students with AD/HD all have different needs and require varied lengths of time to deal with their issues. Depending on a student's needs, the coaching relationship may last from a few months to several years. The average student might expect to spend at least a semester and possibly two to deal with issues and see progress. However, that does not mean that the student may not need to continue working with a coach for several years as other issues arise. Coaching will always be an excellent tool to address problems and deal with AD/HD issues.

The cost of coaching depends on various factors, including where you live and the qualifications of the coach. Standards for AD/HD coaches are now being developed by the Institute for the Advancement of AD/HD Coaching or IAAC (www.adhd coachinstitute.org) and there is an AD/HD Coaches Organization (ACO, www.AD/HDcoaches.org). With this increase in stan-dardization, it should follow that there will be a more stan-dard fee structure. Regardless, be a wise consumer and ask questions. Also, be sure to check to see if coaching is offered at your college. If so, it is usually offered by the counsel-ing center or the Disabled Student Services (DSS) office. Sometimes, it is offered free of charge or for an additional fee for students who qualify as having AD/HD or learning disabilities.

Most coaches charge a monthly fee for services that includes a 30–60 minute weekly face-to-face or phone meeting and sev-eral briefer check-in sessions by email, phone, or text between meetings. In order to compare services, you'll need to know how often you will have contact over the month and compute an hourly rate for services. Or you can ask if the coach has an hourly rate as well.

➥ Extra, Extra!

To learn more about AD/HD coaching, check out these books:

Quinn, P. and Ratey, N. *Coaching college students with AD/HD: Issues and answers*. Washington, DC: Advantage Books.

Ratey, N. *The disorganized mind: Coaching your ADHD brain to take control of your time, tasks, and talents*. New York, NY: St. Martin's Griffin.

Chapter 11
Adding Structure and Achieving Balance

It seems like I'm studying all the time and have no time for other activities. How can I achieve some balance in my life?

If you find that your life is unbalanced and that you are overwhelmed most of the time, that's usually a sign that you need to do something about it. But beware: under- and over-commitments at college can be equally hazardous. Some students with AD/HD have problems with academics, focusing too much on getting it all done, never taking time to relax or socialize. Others take the opposite approach and get so overwhelmed and distracted by all of the social and athletic opportunities that they never get down to really studying (or attending classes regularly). The following suggestions may help you work on achieving some balance in your life:

Balancing academics. When choosing classes it's important to try to achieve balance each semester. That might mean signing up for no more than two classes that require heavy reading and writing or registering for extra classes so that you can drop one or two after you have a chance to attend a few classes to get to know the professor and the assignments. Students who can't seem to set goals for academics and follow through with them may find that they need to work with a coach, advisor, or counselor. Coaching may provide an essential lifeline in providing the structure and accountability that is needed to set goals and stick to them.

Balancing your social life or athletic endeavors. Let's talk about athletics first. Most college programs provide lots of support for their athletes. This includes tutoring, special advising sessions for choosing classes, and supervised study halls. By taking advantage of each of these supports to structure your life, you'll be better able to maintain your academic standing while devoting all of the time necessary to practices, workouts, travel, and games.

Spending too much time socializing is another problem altogether. Most students who engage in social activities to the detriment of their academic success are unaware of what is happening or the consequences until it is often too late. They are enjoying themselves and forget that at college simply showing up once in a while and studying for final exams would yield the results they (or their parents) are looking for. Ending up on academic probation may be the wake-up call that lets them know they need to put some structure into their life. The following answer provides ways to add structure to your day if this is a problem for you as it is for most students with AD/HD.

How can I put some structure into my day?

There are several ways to create structure within the framework of your schedule of classes at college. Most experts on time management, however, offer the same suggestion: start with a master schedule and *schedule everything!*

Create a master schedule. First, complete a weekly schedule that contains *everything* that you do now. This includes classes, travel time, meals, sleep, practices, exercise, screen time (including the internet, social media, and texting) sporting events, meetings, shopping, hair appointments, dating, and partying. Then look at this schedule and find where the open blocks are. This visual is a great way to help you see where you are spending your time and what needs to change.

Now comes the hard work! First, decide what small steps you might take each day to make your life more manageable and balanced to get the results you want. Do you need some more down time each day to do something that you love? Or are you too good at doing what you love and avoiding responsibilities? Let's look at the weekends. Are you spending all of your free time on fun activities and sleeping? Would it be better to schedule some time to catch up or get ahead on assignments?

Now you are ready to make a new, more balanced schedule for next week. Try to create your dream schedule and give it a try. You can continue this process, refining as you go along, until you are happy with the success of the results.

Work. Another way to put structure into your life is to get a part-time job. Now, you might be thinking that you don't have enough time as it is. How is getting a job going to help? You'd be surprised! Over the years I have found that many students with AD/HD have difficulty planning ahead and organizing their time. If they don't have anything to do immediately, at that moment, they tend to not do anything, often procrastinating on projects and assignments. They also seem to think that if they don't have classes on a particular day that they can sleep late and fill the day with other activities rather than reviewing class materials and preparing and completing future assignments. These behaviors quickly become ingrained and over time get them into trouble. Most students with AD/HD do better when they have more to do, forcing them to create a schedule and act accordingly. Part-time work on your days without classes can also do that for you. You will have to get up, be somewhere on time, and get things done. You'll find that you also manage to fit in other things as well. Plus, you'll have some extra spending money! I usually suggest a job on campus that cuts down travel time and also provides you with a supervisor who may be more understanding when you need to take time off for exams or to study for tests.

Get up and get to bed at the same time.   Not having a regular time to get up or go to bed can contribute to lack of structure in your day. Sleeping late robs you of time to work on your academics, attend class, or visit with friends. Also, it is usually one of the reasons that you have to stay up late at night to fit all these activities into your day, thus creating a vicious cycle. Getting enough sleep is usually the key to breaking the cycle (after all, that is why you are sleeping in). Working on sleep, therefore, becomes the key to structuring your day! (See pages 71–79 for more information on getting to bed on time.)

Join an exercise class or a team.   In the same way that having a job and getting up earlier can help bring structure to your life, so can exercise or joining a team. Exercising will give you an added energy boost and is known to decease hyperactivity and restlessness. In addition, participating in a class or on a team—even an intramural team or informal weekly pick-up basketball game—will help give some structure to that day.

⇨ Extra, Extra!

If you need more help documenting where you spend your time, you could try this app:

The Distraction Timer: http://itunes.apple.com/app/ distraction-timer/id395130967?mt=8. This iPhone app keeps track of the actual time you spend on various tasks for a week. It can help you determine how you spend your time so you can make more informed decisions about what needs to change.

How can I control my time on the computer playing games or on Facebook?

All of these activities are by themselves not "bad" and are in fact part of life today. They can become an issue if they are out of control and you find that you are spending time that you are supposed to be working doing something else on the computer. There are ways to get some perspective in all of this. Trying some or all of the following tips may help.

Reward yourself with screen time. Instead of just turning off or delaying use of your favorite devices, use them to reward yourself after studying or doing another chore like cleaning for a specific period of time. Send out a message and let your friends know when you'll be offline and that you won't be answering texts or IMs for a while, then turn off your phone and disable IM chat on your computer. Agree to check in at a certain time after you have finished your work. Without the pressure of looming deadlines or unfinished work, you'll probably enjoy your interactions even more.

Ask your friends. Most likely you are not the only one having this problem. Ask your friends what they do when dealing with electronic distractions. By discussing the problem and working on a solution together, you'll be more likely to stick to a plan if everyone is on board.

⇨ **Extra, Extra!**

If you can't control your screen time on your own, get help! Try the following apps or search for others:

Freedom: http://macfreedom.com. Freedom prevents you from accessing the Internet for up to eight hours at a time. It's available for all operating systems.

Vitamin R: http://www.publicspace.net/Vitamin-R. If the computer-installed solitaire is a distraction for you, just blocking the internet won't do much good. Vitamin R can block software or downloaded applications that are problematic.

Self Control: http://visitsteve.com/made/selfcontrol. Self Control is a Mac-only application that will block your ability to go to specified websites for a period of time.

Work on it with your coach. Bring the problem to your coach and see if you can come up with a solution together. If your coach has worked with other college students, he or she has probably dealt with this issue before. Making a plan and being accountable to another person will help you stay focused on your goal of distraction-free study time.

I can't seem to get my laundry and other boring tasks like cleaning my room done; what can I do?

Most college students struggle with laundry and cleaning, but having AD/HD can make it especially challenging, or challenging in a different way, so the solutions might be a little different for you than for your roommate. There is a way to get a handle on these problems, however, that doesn't involve calling in your mother or paying for a maid service to clean your room.

Put it on your schedule.   With the many competing demands for your time, it's easy to get off-track and put off a task until it just gets too overwhelming to think about. Doing 2 loads of laundry is certainly more manageable than 20! Check your master schedule and look for a time that you can schedule these tasks each week. (See pages 132–133 for creating a master schedule.) Setting up a routine, blocking off the time, and getting in the habit of doing chores a little at a time or in small batches will make them more manageable and more likely to get done. Attacking a molehill is much more manageable then climbing a mountain!

Group boring tasks together.   Doing laundry is a difficult task for someone with AD/HD because you either need to sit and wait (which is boring) or come and go (which means you may forget about it). When you group boring tasks together, you'll be more likely to get them both done. Paying bills, reading study notecards, or completing a reading assignment can all be done while waiting for the wash and dry cycles. You can also listen to notes or an audiobook while tidying your room, hanging up clothes, or grocery shopping.

Do it with a group.   Everybody needs to do their laundry. If you need to be motivated or just want the stimulation of having someone else there with you, try to get together with your friends to get some of the boring tasks done.

Use a body double.   Just as a group can motivate you to get things done, so can a trusted friend. Find someone that you can discuss your particular situation with and see if they are willing to help. A body double may provide the extra bit of motivation you need to tackle a boring project. However, make sure that you chose someone who is not going to be a distraction or get you off-track. For a complete discussion of the use of a body double see the answer to the question that follows.

What is a body double?

In the movies, a body double is an actor who stands in for the leading man or woman during certain shots, but in the world of AD/HD a body double is someone who sits with the person with AD/HD as he tackles tasks that might be difficult to complete alone. Many people with AD/HD find it easier to stay focused on boring tasks when someone else is around to keep them company. The body double may just sit quietly. He may read, listen to music on headphones, or work on the same task that the person with AD/HD is working on. Hard work is simply more fun when someone else is nearby. A body double could be a roommate, a significant other, a sympathetic friend, or another person with AD/HD. Body doubles can be helpful in a wide range of situations including the following:

When you need help with cleaning or doing laundry or any other boring task.   A body double is particularly good for these situations as he or she often offers the incentive to keep going and not give up or get distracted. Having someone to talk with can make the time go more quickly. He or she may also have suggestions for breaking down the task into more manageable sections or for getting the job done more efficiently. Be sure to set up the ground rules for such participation ahead of time, however, so that you don't feel like all your body double is doing is giving advice or nagging. For example, it may be okay for he or she to remind you to get back to the task or to give you encouragement, but not to tell you how to do a task.

When you're working on a project or paper (or any other paperwork). The body double's presence will help keep you from getting distracted. He or she could also offer an occasional encouraging word to keep you motivated to keep working.

When you're determined to stick with an exercise regimen. It's easier to stick to a routine when a body double expects you to show up for workouts. Set up a time to run each morning, or schedule an exercise class together several days a week.

When you're keeping up with daily classwork. Set up a regular time and place to meet with the body double (typically several times a week in a library or another quiet place). If you are late, your body double can call to remind you. The double could be a classmate doing his or her own coursework or a friend who just reads or listens to music on headphones.

When you need help remembering to eat right. College students with AD/HD often forget to stop for meals. Having a set time to eat with friends will help develop a regular routine. You might even go grocery shopping with this body double for food to have on hand in the dorm.

I know I need it, but how do I add structure to my life?

The best way to get a handle on all that you need to do and to add some structure to your day (and life) is to create a master schedule. This schedule can be written down on a white board, a paper day-planner, an electronic online scheduler like Google Calendar, or on your iPhone or iPad. Just make sure that it is large enough to hold *everything* that you need to do each day. That includes classes, study times, eating, exercise, socializing, laundry, errands, shopping, appointments, and a scheduled bedtime. Make sure to also schedule in some down time or breaks to just hang out or have some screen time. Don't forget to set aside 10–15 minutes each day to go over the schedule for the next day.

What kind of planner or organizer is best for students with AD/HD?

No organizing system is perfect and most choices for using a certain planner or organizer are dependent on the needs of the person using them. If they are not designed to meet your needs or are not convenient to use, you will not use them. Period! So, let's look at what some of those needs might be and then you can choose which system you think will work best for you.

• Schedules appointments

• Helps you create a daily master schedule

• Is lightweight, easier to carry around

• Organizes emails, documents, and papers.

• Has space for a "to do" list

• Has alarms and alerts

- Can sync with computer or phone
- Is difficult to lose
- Has a backup file or system
- Comes with as many folders as needed
- Holds all documents, emails, and bills.
- Syncs automatically with other people
- Syncs with electronic "to do" list
- Uses time features to stay on task

In the end, it's up to you. Which system do you think will help you the most? And which system do will think you'll use? At some point you may want to try one out and see if it works for you. Just be sure that you know how your brain processes information best and then choose a system that complements your own internal filing system.

Where and when should I study?

College will offer you many options for studying that you did not have available to you in high school. With no parents around you can choose to study late into the night if you want. Friends or classmates will invite you to study at coffee shops, in study groups, or in the lounge at the dorm. While these choices may all sound appealing at first, it's important to find out what works best for you as early as possible in your college career. Wasted time finding out what works may translate into poor semester grades. The following are tips to help you decide where and when *you* might study best.

Analyze the past.   One way to answer this question is to look back at what worked for you in high school or during a semester

⤷ Extra, Extra!

Here are some sites that will give you more information about scheduling and planning as well as the more popular organizing systems. There are hundreds of thousands of applications out there. Take a look, try a few, and I'm sure you'll find some that can help you become more organized.

ADDvance, "Using a Day Planner as a Life Planner": http://www.addvance.com/add_friendly/daily_planner.html

You Do the Rest: http://www.udotherest.com. A site sponsored by Shire Pharmaceuticals that reviews useful applications for those with AD/HD to help them improve organization and time management, and create notes and memos.

Googlecalendar:http://www.google.com/googlecalendar/about.html.

TeuxDeax: http://www.teuxdeux.com. TeuxDeux is a simple to-do app that has a free browser-based site as well as an iPhone app.

that you did well in college. Think about whether the study environment or time of day was a key factor in whether a study session was a success or not.

Make a list.   List all possible study environments and try to match each with your learning style. (See pages 43–45 for a discussion of learning styles.) Do you need to go to the writing lab to finish that paper? Will music help? Do you need the quiet of the library or will headphones work? Should you exercise first? Do you do better working in a study group discussing the concepts or material with others?

Look at your master schedule. Identify when there are open times for studying. Rate each block and ask yourself if these will work for you. Be honest! Some people really are night owls with their peak attention and alertness after dinner. Others need mornings or afternoons to do more difficult work, because their peak attention occurs earlier in the day. Try to use the time between classes to study or get help while you are on campus. That way you'll have more time in the evening for yourself and other things you need to get done.

Check out your medication. Be sure to take your medication schedule and its duration of action (how long it's effective) into the equation when you are trying to make your decision. Make sure that the times you do choose to study are when your medication is "on board" allowing you to focus and control your inattention and distractibility.

Chapter 12
Understanding How AD/HD Affects Your Relationships and Responsibilities

I'm having problems communicating in my social relationships. Could AD/HD have anything to do with it and what should I do?

Not all students with AD/HD have problems with their social skills, but some do. Poor social skills commonly lead to problems with interpersonal relationships, whether it's getting along with roommates or a boyfriend or girlfriend. Add to the mix problems with anger management, forgetfulness, procrastination, difficulty with decision making, and impulsivity, and you can see why relationships might suffer. But what can you do about it? Here are some ideas.

Identify the problem and any AD/HD symptoms that may be contributing. Knowing that this is a problem area for you is the first step. The reasons for difficulty with making and keeping friends and engaging in social activities may vary from student to student, but usually takes one of two forms. The most common is the loud, often "bossy" person who never stops talking. She is also a poor listener and is constantly thinking about what she is going to say rather than listening to what the other person is saying. As a result, she may interrupt frequently. Without a filter, she may also impulsively say whatever she is thinking, often regretting it immediately. The second scenario involves a student who is withdrawn or shy and extremely uncomfortable in social situations. He may have difficulty joining a group or keeping a conversation going and often avoids social activities altogether.

Make listening a priority. Try to focus on not interrupting. Once you are aware that you have a tendency not to listen and rather to think about what you are going to say, you can make an effort to slow yourself down and focus more on listening. You might also try thinking about a conversation as a game of catch. Only the person with the ball can speak. Therefore, you cannot speak until the other person finishes and throws you the ball. Then it's your turn.

Think about your medication. If you take medication for AD/HD, determine whether it makes a difference in these important communication areas as well. Medication for AD/HD can effectively decrease distractibility and impulsivity and may help you slow down and focus on what is being said. Try to pay attention to how long your medication actually lasts and if you find you interrupt more or are louder when it wears off. To help you better address these problems in social areas, you may need to discuss taking a longer-acting medication or taking your medication on weekends with your healthcare provider.

Ask for help if you need it. Let others know that you are aware that you have problems in certain areas of communication and share that you want to work on them. Ask them to gently let you know if you are interrupting or talking too much. It may help them (and you) to know that you value their friendship and that you are not doing these things on purpose.

By explaining how your AD/HD sometimes makes it impossible for you to "keep still" you are not making an excuse, but sharing that you want to change.

Could AD/HD be affecting my dating and romantic relationships?

Often, young adults with AD/HD do not recognize how their symptoms may affect what is going on in all aspects of their lives. They go from relationship to relationship, never stopping to analyze how AD/HD may be contributing to the problems they experience. Irritability, emotional reactivity, and poor communication skills cannot help but negatively affect the quality of relationships. Impulsivity may cause someone with AD/HD to say things he or she regrets or lead to one break up after another.

Treatment for AD/HD symptoms is critically important to maintaining or improving your dating and romantic relationships. I remember working with one young woman with AD/HD who took forever to realize that she was constantly arguing with her boyfriend on the weekends that she did not take her medication. Once she began taking her medication every day, their relationship became much smoother.

When to disclose your AD/HD in the dating relationship can also be an issue. As with any relationship issue, timing is important. You shouldn't disclose too early, but conversely you shouldn't hide this important part of yourself if a serious relationship has developed. In the beginning, you might just talk about your strengths and weaknesses which would be natural in any relationship. As you feel more comfortable and have lived with each other's vulnerabilities for a while, revealing your AD/HD will be easier as it is an essential part of who you are.

Choice of dating partners may also be affected by AD/HD and its aftermath. Long-standing self-esteem issues may cause you to believe that you are not worthy and choose partners who are not a good match for you. Or you may break up repeatedly or fail to pursue a dating relationship because you perceive that the other person is "too good for me" or "not able to accept me with my problems and failures." Realizing that no one is perfect may help you make better decisions or be willing to stay in relationships longer. Understanding that AD/HD will not go away and that, as a couple, you must confront the daily toll that AD/HD presents, can be the first steps to improving the relationship. Seeking additional individual help or attending couple's therapy, if necessary, can provide additional support and understanding.

Another significant issue may be the contributing role that AD/HD and its aftermath may play in unhealthy or abusive relationships. When assessing your relationship, be on the lookout for subtle clues that things are not going in the right direction. How does your significant other make you feel? Empowered or down on yourself? Accepted and valued for your good qualities or ashamed of your weaknesses? Is this person willing to learn about AD/HD and be part of the solution rather than add to your problems? Instead of blaming and criticizing you, can your significant other work together with you to resolve issues that occur in all relationships? If the answer is no, maybe it is time to get out.

You should also listen to others. What are they saying about this person? Are your friends and family telling you that your significant other is not right for you? Are they telling you there's a problem with the relationship or how you are handling it? Be open, listen carefully, and weigh what they are trying to tell you. They have an outsider's perspective and your judgment may be clouded by your love, impulsivity, or other AD/HD traits. Above all, is the person you are with willing to work on your relationship? Would they consider going with you to therapy to avoid conflicts or deal with other issues you may already have encountered in your relationship? If not, they may not be willing to stick around and work things out after you are married, either. All of this may sound like work, rather than romance, but all rewarding relationships take effort and commitment!

My AD/HD causes me to blurt out things I later regret; what can I do?

The definition of impulsivity is acting or speaking without thinking. Impulsivity is often the main reason for saying and doing things that you later regret. I have often heard impulsivity described as a feeling of having no filters. Whatever comes into your head comes out your mouth. But if it's part of your AD/HD, how can you turn this situation around? One way is to "put on the brakes" and slow down when speaking with others. To address this problem, I would suggest trying to visualize something like a filter or tape across your lips or that your lips are "locked" and you need to go get the "key" before you speak. Both techniques should slow you down enough to ask yourself if the person you are speaking with really wants to hear what you are about to say or if it is appropriate.

You can also step back and analyze when you are more likely to speak out and say something you regret. Is it when you are off your medications, or late in the day when you are tired? Do certain people encourage you to misbehave or say and do things that you later regret? Taking your medication more regularly or avoiding manipulators and their negative influence may help you regain control.

My clutter and messiness is causing "roommate issues," help!

Adolescents with AD/HD often become used to living in a constantly cluttered room at home during high school. Perhaps your parents even gave up on asking you to clean it as long as you kept your door closed. However, unless you have requested a single dorm room, you'll find that at college that you are living with one, two, or even three roommates and they may not be as tolerant of your mess and clutter! So what can you do? First, you'll need to get control. AD/HD clutter tends to multiply! If you haven't done your laundry for weeks or emptied your trash, you're more likely to just toss today's dirty clothes on top of the pile and let the clutter grow. There are no easy answers, but before you tackle existing clutter, start by creating no "new" clutter. Get in the habit of always putting your shoes in the closet, hanging your coat where it belongs, and throwing trash away immediately, rather than putting it on the desk or leaving wrappers and pizza boxes all over the room. Be kind to yourself and tackle as much as you can handle. Try to focus on one action per day and go from there! Now let's make a plan to attack the clutter that's accumulated.

Think small. Don't take on too much at once—take on the stack of magazines or empty food containers or "one drawer per day" or "one shelf per day" and then reward yourself for your accomplishment.

Finish what you start. Take on one small organizing project at a time and then stick with it to completion. Make it enjoyable! Add music or your favorite TV show and you have a half-hour or hour chunk of time to help you focus and stick to a task. Match boring tasks to ones that you enjoy. Folding laundry while watching TV makes the task less onerous.

Don't try to do it alone. You or your friends can work on this together. Ask your friends for ideas that might help with your clutter, or for support in digging out your room. What do they do to get their laundry done or clothes put away? Support each other in a non-critical way and provide the incentive to get the task done! Understand that being organized with AD/HD doesn't come naturally, but with help you can do it.

Money management (particularly overspending) is a serious problem for me. Does that have anything to do with my AD/HD?

Problems with money management are common for college students (and many adults) with AD/HD. It's easy to get into financial difficulty at college because you'll now be spending without any supervision. Credit cards make spending too easy, particularly if you are impulsive. Here are some tips to help get your spending under control.

Consider switching to cash. This is often a good solution for students with AD/HD as paper bills allow them to concretely see how much money they have and how it dwindles as they spend their cash. To make this plan work, you'll need to determine how much you have to spend each week and withdraw that amount from your account at the beginning of the week. If you find that by the end of the week you continually have spent all your cash and need more, it may signal that you need to reassess your spending habits or your budget.

Freeze your cards. Literally! Take credit cards and float them in a plastic container of water and put it in the freezer. Do not unthaw them until your debt is cleared or your spending habits are under control. It you feel this will not work for you, contact the credit card company and ask them to put a hold on the card or decline all purchases.

Check in with your bank. Most banks have personnel who will help you set up a budget or deal with credit card debt. Stop in for a visit or call to see if anyone can help. Many campuses have a bank branch on campus as well.

Look for workshops. There may be workshops on handling finances held on campus or in the community. These workshops can help you assess what is going on and work on getting your finances under control.

Target specific problems. Look at where your spending is out of control. Phone bills, online shopping, not paying bills on time, or excessive credit card spending are common areas that get students in trouble. Once you've identified the problem, set up a plan to make changes. Your coach, campus counselor, or bank employees are resources that can help you develop a workable plan.

Look for ways to earn money. Consider getting a part-time job on campus, tutoring, babysitting, or becoming an RA to earn money to reduce your accumulated debt, pay routine bills, or give you some extra spending money.

Talk with the financial aid office. Explore student loans and tuition payment plans.

Use apps for tracking your spending and bank account status. Most systems include alerts that will let you know when bills are due or when you are approaching your spending limit.

Bank online. Setting up an online account may enable you to pay bills, check your financial status more regularly, and help you to avoid late fees.

Set up a budget. This probably is one of the most important steps that you can take to get a realistic picture of your financial status and to rein in spending. It will also give you a tool that will help you achieve your goals later in life, whether it's buying a car or your first house.

Assess for addiction. Individuals with AD/HD, because of their impulsivity and other symptoms, are at risk for shopping, spending, or gambling addictions. If you feel out of control and none of the things you have tried or promises you have made seem to be working, you may have a problem in this area. Make an appointment at the counseling center as soon as you can to assess whether your problems in these areas need a more intensive solution.

I have many other responsibilities while attending college, including work and a family. How can I do it all?

You can't! That's why you'll need to plan to ask for help and to take extra care of yourself! To try to achieve a good balance in your life, be sure to write everything on your master schedule, and don't take on too much. (See pages 132–133 for how to

⮌ **Extra, Extra!**

For more information about money management, check out:

Moulton Sarkis, S. and Klein, K. *ADD and your money: A guide to personal finance for adults with Attention Deficit Disorder.* Oakland, CA: New Harbinger Publications.

You could also try using an online personal finance tool, like Mint: http://www.mint.com. Mint allows you track and categorize your expenses, create personal spending charts, and calculate personalized budgets. It has free smartphone apps as well.

create a master schedule.) Remember the story of the Tortoise and the Hare and take a reduced course load. It may take you longer to graduate, but you'll be more likely to reach the finish line. You might consider taking some of your classes online. That will cut down on travel time and afford you more flexibility. And lastly, find a quiet place to do classwork. You may find, not surprisingly, that it's not at home.

The most important advice I can give is to urge you to ask for help and support from others. The following action plan will get everyone on the same page and working together. It doesn't take much for life to get a little chaotic—or for home life to intrude on your study time. Here are several ways to minimize the stress on everyone.

1. Post your schedule, including study time, on the family calendar so everyone knows when you're available—and when you're not.

2. Before classes start, discuss changing roles and expectations with family members, especially your significant other.

3. Redistribute household chores such as laundry, meal preparation, and cleaning.

4. Arrange for carpools and after-school child care if needed.

5. Remove yourself from the home environment to study.

6. Sleep eight hours, if possible, and exercise regularly to decrease stress.

7. Consider seeing a therapist for support. Stepping back from your role as caretaker may be more challenging than classwork. A therapist can help you make the transition from work or home to school.

Chapter 13
Deciding Whether to Stay in or Drop out

This was my first-choice school, but it isn't working! What should I do if my current school isn't a good fit?

If you have been following your plan for success (see page 35) and you're continuing to struggle at your current placement, transferring out or taking some time off may be in your best interest. An important consideration, however, is to make sure that you have fully assessed your current situation so that you won't continue to have the same issues whatever you decide to do. In order to ensure success, consider the following:

Take an honest look at why things aren't working for you.
Is it your skills? Your program? Your choices? Are you just having adjustment issues that will eventually resolve? Make a list of issues you are having and why you think they have resulted in such dissatisfaction (after all, you thought this was the school for you at some point). Now is a good time to reflect honestly about what you have learned about yourself, your strengths and weaknesses, and to work on your self-advocacy skills. Then discuss your problems with an objective person and get their take on what is going on that may be standing in your way of success. If you conclude that your current environment cannot meet your needs, it's time to look for another placement. Transferring to another school is discussed below and in the following question on page 158.

Find the best match possible.   Look at the requirements for admission at that institution. Some schools may have requirements that may be too rigorous or in other ways not be right for you to ensure success. Make sure you can get your needs met at any placement you might choose. Consider schools that offer individual attention for you to be successful or colleges that have services for students with disabilities.

Take a leave of absence.   Instead of transferring, use this time to work on skills, then come back to your first choice college. Don't look at this as a failure but as a way to get things back on track. (See pages 164–165 for a discussion of withdrawal.)

Consider taking a gap year.   One of the biggest fears parents have is that their children will not go back to college after a gap year. But not only do most students go back to college, students often come back more focused and refreshed, more mature, and often do better academically. Gap year advocates have long maintained that taking time off can benefit students, who use the time to figure out what they want from their college educations, and have the opportunity to check out careers without making huge commitments of time or money.

When should I transfer out?

When your situation or school isn't a good match for you or isn't meeting your needs, and before your grades interfere with acceptance at another institution, consider transferring to a more appropriate placement. But remember, simple geographic moves are not always the answer. Transferring to another school without assessing your needs and what went wrong in your current placement will not produce different results. To avoid making the same mistake, consider your next placement carefully.

What placement options should I consider?

Before you begin to consider each option, take a few minutes to reflect on your current situation.

Make a list of accommodations and services that worked for you. Consider these accommodations essential at your next placement.

Take a look at your unmet needs. Make a list of these as well. This list may actually be more important as it most likely contains the main reasons your current placement did not work out for you. After you have done this, the following are options you might consider.

Look for a comparable school with a strong support program or one that meets your needs in other areas. These needs might include a particular course, major, or geographic location that you cannot get at your current placement.

Consider a two-year degree or a community college closer to home and your support systems. Many students miss the supports they have been used to and have difficulty finding their way in a large four-year program. It's great if you can realize this early and transfer to a program that will support you and allow you to stretch and grow at your own pace. For some students, a four-year program is just too long to sustain their interest or effort and transferring to a two-year degree will allow them to develop skills and try out a particular area of interest. They may then choose to go on in a particular field or earn a four-year degree later.

Try an internship, work-study program, or study abroad. Most universities offer internships, work-study, or study abroad programs. If you are not sure about your major, or want to take a break from academics and live in the real world for a while, these can provide great opportunities. They are also a great way to help you decide on the path or career you want to pursue.

Pursue an online degree.   Many students with AD/HD find that the flexibility of pursuing a degree online is just what they need. They can study and attend classes late into the night or while their medication is effective. Online classes have fewer distractions and provide a lot of structure. They are also great for more visual learners. You may need to be very disciplined to stay focused, however. Working with a coach can often help in this area.

Attend a college for students with disabilities.   While there are only a handful of these programs, they provide an opportunity for students with severe disabilities or those newly diagnosed with AD/HD who have not had time to adjust to their disabilities before college an opportunity to be successful during their first attempt at the college experience. These programs provide college-level courses, as well as remedial services, coaching, tutoring, other supports. In these programs, students learn about themselves, their learning styles, and gain confidence along with college credits. Upon completion of the program, students often transfer to four-year institutions with the knowledge and background necessary for success.

➥ Extra, Extra!

Here are two colleges with specially designed programs for students with AD/HD and LD:

Beacon College: http://www.beaconcollege.edu

Landmark College: http://www.landmark.edu

What type of college is best for students with AD/HD?

No one type of institution is preferable for students with AD/HD. Success at college depends on several factors, including the school's knowledge of AD/HD and how it affects students, the support programs it offers, and the willingness of its faculty to help students succeed. Knowledge of your needs will allow you to be better prepared to determine whether a particular program is right for you. (See the needs assessment on page 112.) Most colleges offer some type of support. Some are just better at it and further along than others. That's where an established program with well-trained personnel comes in. A program may look good on paper or in a guide to colleges for students with disabilities, but the current staff are the ones who make the program run smoothly. Be a wise consumer (college costs are high!) and make sure you get what you are paying for. When you are considering a college, make sure that you ask to talk with other students with AD/HD so that you can get a sense of how the program works on that campus.

I'm doing better now that I know I have AD/HD and it is being treated. How can I transfer into my first-choice school?

If you were not able to get into your first-choice school initially, but after addressing your AD/HD and getting treatment and accommodations, you have a year of strong grades and want to transfer, go for it! But, do your homework! Check out the transfer process and the requirements for admission and start the process as early as possible. By waiting, you may be too late and there may not be enough spaces or time before the applications close.

It's important to reexamine your first-choice school and make sure that it has a program that will meet all of your needs. Does it provide the same services that you are currently receiving that contributed to your success? Will all of your credits transfer? (You worked hard for them!) Is the tuition comparable or worth the increase? Does it have the major you are looking for? Transfer students can have their own unique challenges, so find out what is offered for orientation and support activities.

Although there may be many good reasons for transferring, there may also be disadvantages (making new friends, finding your way, and finding resources and contacts for services). Make sure that you weigh them all. You decided on your first-choice school *before* attending college. You are not the same person who made that decision. After additional reflection, many students decide that they like their courses, the friends they have made, and the success that they have had and choose to stay where they are.

Should I drop out?

This is a question that's difficult to answer, as the reasons for asking it may be as varied as the persons asking. "Dropping out" suggests that you are just "walking away" or "giving up" on the idea of college. However, poor grades or limited finances may make it impossible at this point in time to accomplish what you set out to do. That doesn't mean that you should abandon your plans, however. Rather than seeing yourself as a failure and feeling that you must now "quit" or "give up" (all negative messages suggested by the term "dropping out"), take a pointer from the military. When troops are forced back by the enemy, instead of referring to this fallback position as a "retreat," they prefer to think of it as a "strategic redeployment" of the troops to gain a better advantage later on. There are several points to consider before doing this, however.

Reframe your situation, then look for a solution. You can do this by realistically assessing what went wrong. Were you prepared for the differences you found at college? Did you have all the skills you need to be successful? Did you attend class and keep up with assignments or did you party and forget about your responsibilities? Did you access accommodations and ask for help when you needed it? Did you take your medication? Was this placement the right choice for you? Why not?

Look at your options. If the semester is not over (that is, if classes are still in session and no final exams have taken place), can you withdraw or "stop out" rather than "drop out?" (See pages 164–165 for a discussion of withdrawal and stopping out.) Can you apply for student loans or make other financial arrangements? Can you work and still go to school part-time?

Make a plan. Instead of just walking away, now that you have a better idea of what went wrong, make an appointment with your advisor to discuss your options. Then make a plan. This plan may involve "stepping away" or "changing direction" from the path you are on right now, but should not preclude returning at some point in the future when your situation allows for it.

SOS! I'm already in trouble this semester; what should I do?

First, don't panic! There is a lot that you can do right now to turn the situation around.

Talk to someone. Consult your professor or advisor—as soon as possible! Drop in during their office hours or schedule an appointment to meet.

Analyze your options. What is the add/drop deadline? Can you drop the class you are having the most difficulty in? Can you ask to do extra credit to bring up your grades? Can you take an Incomplete? Should you consider requesting a withdrawal for the semester? (See the question and answer below that discusses withdrawal as an option.) Did you overcommit this semester and should you consider reducing your course load? (See pages 165–167) for a discussion of taking a reduced course load.) By reducing your course load to 12 hours, you can still be considered a full-time student, but have less work to focus on. Or should you drop back to nine credits or less and go to school part-time?

Find a permanent solution. Whatever you choose to do right now, remember that it is only an interim fix. You still need to analyze why you got into trouble in the first place.

How and when should I request a withdrawal?

If it is in your best interest or if you are unable to complete the courses you began in a given semester, you should consider initiating the formal procedure to request a withdrawal from college for the remainder of the semester. Doing this earlier in the semester typically allows you to withdraw without academic penalty (grades being recorded) and to get back some of your tuition money. Absence from classes *does not* constitute a withdrawal, and absences that continue through final exams may result in failing grades. Failure to follow proper withdrawal procedures may produce results, such as poor or failing grades, that make it difficult for you to return to your current college or to transfer to another college or university. You will also have a continuing financial obligation for the semester if you do not formally withdraw.

If you are ready to return to school the semester following the one in which you withdrew, be sure to check with the college as each college has detailed procedures for re-entering. If you decide not to return or to transfer to another institution the following semester, initiating formal withdrawal procedures from your present placement is important. If you have already registered at your present college for the subsequent semester, it is your obligation to clear these course enrollments. No matter what you are considering, it's best to discuss your plans with an advisor, professor, assistant dean, and your parents. At some colleges, students in good standing or on probation may also have the option, depending on college rules, of "stopping out" or taking a leave of absence for a time; that is, leaving college for one or two semesters without initiating formal withdrawal procedures. Students who have stopped out will need to contact the admissions department to be reinstated and to receive a registration eligibility time.

What about a reduced course load?

Some students with AD/HD decide not to attend college full-time, either at first or at some point in their college experience. Part-time typically means that the student takes only 2 or 3 classes (9 hours or less of classes) instead of a full course load of 4 to 5 (12 to 15 hours). Most four-year colleges will not allow a student to attend part-time during their entire academic career and live in the dormitory. However, they may allow for some portion of the degree to be earned as a part-time student. There may be many reasons for this arrangement. Some students find being in college so taxing because of their learning and attention disabilities that they need more variety and balance in their lives. Most colleges have a provision for requesting a temporary underload for a semester for any student experiencing an extenuating circumstance. Additionally, some colleges list a course underload as a possible accommodation based on a student's disability. When taking this approach, attending summer sessions to stay on track for graduation may be required. Others may attend college part-time for a semester or a year if they have to work longer hours (more than 15 hours of work per week usually qualifies a student for part-time status); if they have emotional or substance abuse issues that require treatment; if they or a family member have a medical crisis; if they have responsibilities for taking care of a child or a family member; or for financial reasons. The Office of Student Financial Aid can provide information for you concerning possible partial adjustment of tuition and fees if you decide to attend with a reduced course load.

Does a reduced course load affect financial aid?

Most financial aid is dependent on your being a full-time student. A reduced course load can affect financial aid, but that depends on the institution. Be sure to check out the number of credits required per semester to continue eligibility when you apply for aid or if you are considering dropping a course or going part-time. Students on academic probation may also have financial aid affected. Contact the Office of Student Financial Aid for more information. Of course, if you take a reduced course load you will inevitably need to attend college for additional semesters, so the costs will also be higher and you will need to plan for this even if you are not on financial aid.

How do I deal with academic probation?

Many students with AD/HD experience some form of academic difficulty during their college career. Some students may simply struggle through a class or two or for a single term. For others, academic difficulty may be more severe or long-lasting. Whatever the situation, there are many ways to connect with staff, faculty, and fellow students that may help you overcome the difficulties you have been experiencing. Make sure you seek help as soon as you know you are in trouble.

In most schools students are placed on academic probation when their cumulative GPA (grade point average) falls below 2.0 or when their term GPA falls below 1.5 (even if their cumulative GPA remains above 2.0). Students who are on a 2.0 probation have the following semester to raise their cumulative average. Students who are on term probation usually must gain a 2.0 GPA for the following term and maintain a cumulative 2.0. Students who do not clear academic probation by the end of their probationary semester are usually subject to dismissal, but may appeal the decision.

As a student on academic probation, the two most important steps you can take are to gain as much information as possible about your individual academic situation and, based on this information, develop a plan to return to good academic standing in the following semester. This is the time to do the following:

Learn about your school's procedures. First, assess the severity of your grade point average deficit. Be aware of the grades needed to clear probationary status and what procedures you will need to follow.

Know what courses you should be taking or retaking. While I often suggest repeating all courses in which you received a D or an F, not all colleges allow this to happen, so you'll need to check to see what the policy is on repeating a course. Additionally, it is not advisable to repeat a course in which you received a D if it is not required for a major or is no longer of interest to you. D grades, while not preferable, are passing grades.

Develop a new study schedule and routine. This will provide you with both the structure and support you need to concentrate on improving your academic performance. Clearly what you were doing in the past did not produce the results you wanted. Now is the time to analyze your previous study strategies and routine and make any necessary changes. Set SMART goals (see pages 36–37) regarding the amount of time you'll devote to studying and stick to them. Decide where and when you study best (see pages 141–143) and carefully assess all courses you enroll in for the next semester. Consider whether you need to employ a tutor or a coach to keep you on track. Many colleges offer supervised study halls for athletes and others. You might inquire to see if you could join such a program.

Seek academic advising. When placed on probation, the first person you should notify is your academic advisor, so drop in or schedule an appointment as soon as possible. Ask your advisor what else he or she suggests you do to improve your academic standing. This may also be an important time to rethink your major. Many times students' grades suffer because they have selected a major that is not really matched to their strengths. Keep an open mind and consider whether there is a better major for you. (It may also be good to let your parents know what is going on as well, but you may want to wait until you have a plan of action for dealing with probation that you can present to them.)

Make use of resources.   Visit the Disabled Student Services (DSS) office to ensure that you are making use of all of the resources that your college has to offer. (See page 107 for more information about specialized services that might be available to you.)

Reduce your course load.   Students who work 15 hours or more or who have a documented disability may be able to reduce their course load below the 12 hours required for full-time student status. See if this option would be a good possibility for you.

Set your priorities.   In addition to seeing your advisor and accessing support services, you'll also need to do a serious assessment of your other commitments. Passing your classes should now become your number one priority. Be honest with yourself about your other commitments, and, as hard as it may be, cut out as much as you need to in order to make sure your academics are getting the time and attention they deserve. After all, you can't be involved in all you want to do if you're not allowed back in school next semester. Make a list of what you need to do (like working) versus what you want to do (like having fun with your friends) and make some changes as needed.

I'm an adult returning to college after having dropped out earlier. What can I do to be successful this time around?

Congratulations! You have lots of experience to draw on to help you answer this question. Most likely you were unaware of your AD/HD during your past college experience. Even though you met with failure in the past, don't assume that it's going to be the same this time. You have made lots of advances and so has college. However, there are a few assignments that may help. Take a look at the following:

Analyze what went wrong in the past. Knowing that you have AD/HD and how it affects the way you learn will help you to complete coursework and assignments and hand them in on time. Think back on your last school experience. What types of work gave you trouble? Were lectures particularly difficult? Tests? Long-term assignments? In which classes were you able to do your best work? Assess your strengths and weaknesses and aim for classes that balance your workload in favor of your strengths. (See pages 40–43 for a discussion of strengths and weaknesses.)

Find out what types of assignments each department— and each instructor—generally gives. If writing long essays is problematic for you, limit the number of classes that will require lengthy reports. If lectures are difficult for you to follow, don't load up on them in a single semester and bring along a device such as a tape recorder or Pulse Smart pen. (See page 116 for information about the Pulse Smart pen.)

Call on your life and work experiences. They will help you a lot at college. Some universities will even give you credits for these experiences. You've probably learned a lot about working with others and asking for help. In addition, you are more mature and may have other responsibilities now. Your priorities may have changed and you may be more focused on learning. Be sure to use all of these resources when choosing classes and seeking help.

Choose your major wisely. Remember, you get to pick your major and can follow your passions. Sure, you'll have to take certain required courses, but much of what you'll study will be what you *want* to study. You're also free to dabble in things that interest you—anything from pottery to fencing to the study of ancient civilizations—just for the fun of it. You are most likely back at college after work, so make use of your real-world experiences to help you choose what you want to do.

Get whatever help is available and get it early. Find out what services may be available to students with disabilities and what documents you'll need to receive them. Consider seeking accommodations such as note takers, extended time for tests, the use of your school's writing center, and access to peer tutors. Formal or informal study groups may also be available. Would hiring a coach help? Do whatever works.

Take advantage of orientations and non-credit courses in time management and study skills that are offered at many colleges and universities.

Gather the right tools. Pick the calendar or day planner you know works best for you and carry it with you, even when you're not heading for class. You'll need to integrate other activities—

work, social life, family life—around your school schedule. (See question on page 153 that addresses this topic.) Buy a small tape recorder or Pulse Smart pen for recording lectures and other classes. Toss a few highlighters into your bag. Since you, not the school, own your books now, you can feel free to mark them up in any way that helps you keep track of important information. If you've got a heavy reading load, see which books on your list are available in audio format and rent them, if that helps you.

Make friends.   Get to know classmates, especially those who appear to have their acts together. Get their phone numbers or email addresses so you'll be able to contact them to clarify assignments when necessary. Join or form your own study groups.

Get support from home.   If you are a parent or have other family responsibilities, ask family members for help. Discuss your academic goals with your family and work out a plan to share household chores and other responsibilities. A specific game plan will help you address your family's needs during those times you are at school or studying. (See page 153.)

Consider an AD/HD coach.   An AD/HD coach can tailor her support of your academic efforts in a way that's as individual as your needs. For instance, a coach can help you to:

- Manage personal activities such as getting enough sleep and exercise and doing laundry.
- Structure plans for addressing long-term assignments.
- Improve self-esteem and decrease negative thoughts.
- Help you identify successful strategies for learning.

Consider taking medication.   If you were not diagnosed the last time you were at college, but are now, be sure to consider taking or beginning medication for AD/HD. Your back-to-school plans inevitably will change some of your activity patterns, such as staying up later than usual to study. Inform your physician of your school plans so that he or she can work with you to create a treatment regimen that reduces AD/HD symptoms with minimal side effects. AD/HD is a 24-hour-a-day disorder, but when and how you medicate should address your needs and schedule. While you may not have taken medication the last time you were at college, new demands and the pressures of college may change your needs. Discuss with your physician the possibility of starting a medication program that takes your school plans into account.

By addressing how your AD/HD will impact your academic career early, you will have a better chance for developing coping strategies. And better strategies will go a long way toward academic success this time around.

Chapter 14
Other Important Issues

Should I work while I'm in college?

Sometimes this choice is not an option, but is made out of neces-
sity for financial reasons, either to pay tuition—although most
colleges have financial aid options, so that students and their
families can get support or loans for college—or, for some
students, to support their family. If you need to work make sure
that you are realistic about what you can accomplish in a day.
This may be the time to reduce your course load or attend college
part-time. If you have to work, you might also consider getting
a job on campus. It might not pay as well but the convenience
to classes and the likelihood that you will have a supervisor that
understands when you need to request time off for study may be
worth the trade-off. In addition, you'll still be on campus and
can use to the opportunity to make friends.

For some students with AD/HD, I do recommend that they
get a part-time job while at college to add structure to their day
(plus, it can have the added advantage of giving them some
extra spending money!). Students with AD/HD often do better
when functioning on a full schedule. If they have nothing to do
(a day without classes), they do nothing! The more they have
to do, the more efficient they become. You may have experienced this phenomenon during high school when you had after
school sports or other activities and little time in the evening
except to study and get to bed. Although many students dislike

or resist this option, later they readily admit that they benefited by being in the "real world" and seeing the truth about having a job, and that they came to a better appreciation for why they were at college. However, if you have significant learning differences that impact your academics and require that you spend extra time studying or with a tutor, I strongly recommend against working.

I'm having difficulty choosing a major; how can I decide?

If you're like many of the college students with AD/HD that I have worked with, you have probably changed your major at least once already. Similarly, many of you will have such varied interests that picking a career path may be difficult. Students with AD/HD often change their major as they take a particular course or attend a lecture that captures their imagination. The following are suggestions to help you narrow your choices.

Look to your strengths. Experts agree that the best way to choose a major or to assess a career is to look for one based on your strengths. (See pages 40–43 to find out how to determine your strengths).

Major in something that you're interested in. Look at the course catalog and see what classes you're drawn to (as opposed to what will help you get a job); you might find that what you want to take isn't what you thought you'd end up doing.

Ask for help. If you are having a particularly difficult time deciding on a major, visit the career counseling center on campus. The staff are professionals trained to assist students in this process each year and may have ideas and suggestions that you have not thought of.

Get tested. Testing can identify careers that suit your personality—and can eliminate those careers that may sound great, but don't mesh with your personality or abilities. Testing may include an interest and a personality inventory as well as an abilities test. These tests are fun to take and may come up with careers that you haven't even thought of.

Choose a couple of broad areas. After you have gathered information, choose a couple of broad areas that interest you and take a class in each. If you are still interested, talk to someone in the field and gather as much information as you can. You might even consider taking an internship or getting a summer job in that area before declaring it as a major.

Avoid using a process of elimination. Whatever you do, don't use a process of elimination to choose your major. Eliminating what you are not good at may mean that you end up choosing something that you are not particularly interested in and eventually end up in a career that you don't like. Instead choose based on your strengths and interests.

Are any majors better for students with AD/HD?

In addition to assessing and deciding on a major based on your strengths as outlined above, the most important advice I can give students with AD/HD is to encourage them to look into careers and majors that they feel passionate about. Careers that offer stimulation and changing schedules are best, as are careers that provide an outlet for creativity and "out of the box" thinking. Careers that require excellent organization or repetitive skills should be avoided. However, I find that people with AD/HD can do whatever they set their minds to if they are motivated and passionate. So after reflection, try to follow your passion! You'll be rewarded in satisfaction, if not monetarily.

I'm having problems with drugs and alcohol. Is there a connection between AD/HD and addiction?

Symptoms of AD/HD combined with situations at college can expose students to considerable risk for abusing substances. Students with AD/HD are often under stress and suffer from depression. The use of alcohol or drugs may be seen as a way to reduce stress and may be socially or emotionally rewarding. For a person with AD/HD, the combination of impulsivity, poor self-esteem, freedom from supervision, and easy access to various substances may be extremely dangerous. Most students do not intend to become abusers when they begin. Treatment of AD/HD with stimulant medication in childhood, however, has been shown to result in a decrease in these behaviors and to reduce the risk of substance abuse in adolescence and adulthood. Studies have shown that individuals with untreated AD/HD are at three to four times greater risk for alcohol and substance use disorder (Wilens, et al., 2003; Biederman, 2003).

A Few Final Words

Gaining a fuller understanding of your AD/HD and how it affects you is the single most important factor in its successful management. Self-knowledge will then lead to self-advocacy and is the key to securing the exact accommodations for your learning needs at college. While the parents of young children with AD/HD are often the ones who pursue this information, being on your own as a young adult necessitates that you take responsibility for your AD/HD and develop a program that meets your needs. Such a program usually includes medication, individual therapy, learning accommodations, counseling, coaching, and other supports. Living a healthy lifestyle will help you look and feel great, and making AD/HD-friendly choices will empower you to live well despite your AD/HD. The college years provide each of you with a wonderful opportunity for individual growth. Here's hoping that you find the answers to your more important questions along the way. If not, keep asking until you do. Good luck!

References

Arnold, L. E., Kleykaml, D., Votolato, N., Gibson, R.A., & Horrocks, L. (1994). Potential link between dietary intake of fatty acids and behavior: Pilot exploration of serum lipids in attention-deficit hyperactivity disorder. *Journal of Child and Adolescent Psychopharmacology, 4,* 171–182.

Barkley, R., Murphy, K., & Kwasnick, D. (1996). Vehicle driving competencies and risk in teens and young adults with attention deficit hyperactivity disorder. *Pediatrics, 98,* 1089–1095.

Biederman J. (2003). Pharmacotherapy for attention-deficit/hyperactivity disorder (ADHD) decreases the risk for substance abuse: Findings from a longitudinal follow-up of youths with and without ADHD. *Journal of Clinical Psychiatry, 64,* Suppl 11, 3–8.

Biederman, J., Ball, S. W., Monuteaux, M. C., Surman, C. B., Johnson, J. L., & Zeitlin, S. (2007). Are girls with ADHD at risk for eating disorders? Results from a controlled, five-year prospective study. *Journal of Developmental and Behavioral Pediatrics, 28*(4) 302–307.

Biederman, J., Faraone, S., Spenser, T., Wilens, T., Norman, D., Lapey, K., . . . Doyle, A. (1993). Patterns of psychiatry comorbidity, cognition, and psychosocial functioning in adults with attention deficit hyperactivity disorder. *American Journal of Psychiatry, 150,* 1792–1798.

Black, D.S., Milam, J, & Sussman, S. (2009). Sitting-meditation interventions among youth: A review of treatment efficacy. *Pediatrics, 124,* e532–41.

Bouchard, M.F., Bellinger, D.C., Wright, R.O., & Weisskopf, M.G. (2010). Attention-deficit/hyperactivity disorder and urinary metabolites of organophosphate pesticides. *Pediatrics, 125,* e1270–7.

Brown, T.E., Reichel, P.C. & Quinlan, D.M. (2011). Executive function impairments in high IQ children and adolescents with ADHD. *Open Journal of Psychiatry, 1,* 56–65.

Dukarm, C. (2005). Bulimia nervosa and ADD: A possible role for stimulant medication. *Journal of Women's Health, 14,* 345–350.

Dukarm, C. (2006). *Pieces of the puzzle: A link between eating disorders and AD/HD.* Washington, DC: Advantage Books.

Field, S., Parker, D., Sawilowsky, S., & Rolands, L. (2010). *Quantifying the effectiveness of coaching for college students with attention deficit/hyperactivity disorder: Final report to the Edge Foundation.* Retrieved from http://www.edgefoundation.org/wp-content/uploads/2011/01/Edge-Foundation-ADHD-Coaching-Research-Report.pdf

Fredrickson, B. L., & Branigan, C. (2005). Positive emotions broaden the scope of attention and thought-action repertoires. *Cognition and Emotion, 19,* 313–332.

Haffner J., Roos J., Goldstein N., Parzer P., & Resch, F. (2006). The effectiveness of body-oriented methods of therapy in the treatment of attention-deficit hyperactivity disorder (ADHD): Results of a controlled pilot study. *Z Kinder Jugendpsychiatr Psychother, 34,* 37–47.

Jensen P.S. & Kenny, D.T. (2004). The effects of yoga on the attention and behavior of boys with attention-deficit/ hyperactivity disorder (ADHD). *Journal of Attention Disorders, 7,* 205–16.

Jerome, L., Habinski, L., & Segal, A. (2006). Attention-deficit/ hyperactivity disorder (ADHD) and driving risk: A review of the literature and a methodological critique. *Current Psychiatry Report, 8,* 416–426.

Johnson, M., Ostlund, S., Fransson, G., Kadeyo, B., & Gielberg, C. (2009). Omega-3/omega-6 fatty acids for attention deficit hyperactivity disorder: A randomized placebo-controlled trial in children and adolescents. *Journal of Attention Disorders, 12,* 394–401.

Klingberg, T., Fernell, E., Olesen, P., Johnson, M., Gustafsson, P., Dahlström, K., . . . Westerberg, H. (2005). Computerized training of working memory in children with AD/HD: A randomized, controlled trial. *Journal of the American Academy of Child and Adolescent Psychiatry, 44,* 177–186

Mikami, A.Y., Hinshaw, S.P., Patterson, K.A., & Lee, J.C. (2008). Eating pathology among adolescent girls with attention-deficit/ hyperactivity disorder. *Journal of Abnormal Psychology, 117,* 225–235.

National Center for Education Statistics, U.S. Department of Education. (2000). *Postsecondary students with disabilities: Enrollment, services and persistence* (NCES 2000–092). Retrieved from http:// nces.ed.gov/pubs2000/2000092.pdf

National Center for Education Statistics, U.S. Department of Education. (2003). *CD-ROM: Beginning postsecondary students longitudinal study: Second follow-up Data Analysis System (DAS) BPS:96/01* (Tables on degree attainment and persistence of 1995–96 beginning postsecondary students in 2001 by disability status and learning disability status). Retrieved from http://nces.ed.gov/ pubsearch/pubsinfo.asp?pubid=2003159

Newman, L., Wagner, M., Cameto, R., & Knokey, A. M. (2009). *The post-high school outcomes of youth with disabilities up to 4 years after high school: A report from the National Longitudinal Transition Study–2 (NLTS2)* (NCSER 2009–3017). Retrieved from www.nlts2.org/reports/2009_04/nlts2_report_2009_04_ complete.pdf

Nigg, J.T., Lewis, K., Edinger, T. & Falk, M. (2012). Meta-analysis of attention-deficit/hyperactivity disorder or attention-deficit/ hyperactivity disorder symptoms, restriction diet, and synthetic food color additives. *Journal of the American Academy of Child and Adolescent Psychiatry, 51*, 86–97.

Rabiner, D.L., Anastopoulous, A.D., Costello, J., Hoyle, R., & Swartzwelder, H.S. (2008). Adjustment to college in students with AD/HD. *Journal of Attention Disorders, 11*, 689–699.

Ramsey, J.R., & Rostain, A. (2005). Adapting psychotherapy to meet the needs of adults with attention-deficit/hyperactivity disorder. *Psychotherapy: Theory, Research, Practice and Training, 42*, 72–84.

Ratey, J. (2008). *Spark: The revolutionary new science of exercise and the brain.* New York, NY: Little, Brown and Company.

Surman, C., Randall, E., & Biederman, J. (2006). Is there an association between AD/HD and bulimia? *Journal of Clinical Psychiatry, 67*, 351–354.

Surman, C. P., Adamson, J.J., Petty, C., Biederman, J., Kenealy, D. C., Levine, M., . . . Faraone, S. V. (2009). Association between attention-deficit/hyperactivity disorder and sleep impairment in adulthood: Evidence from a large controlled study. *Journal of Clinical Psychology, 70*, 1523–1529.

Weber, W., Vander Stoep, A., McCarty, R. L., Weiss, N. S., Biederman, J., & McClellan, J. (2008). Hypericum perforatum (St. John's wort) for attention-deficit/hyperactivity disorder in children and adolescents: A randomized controlled trial. *Journal of the American Medical Association, 299*, 2633–41.

Wilens, T. E, Faraone, S. V., Biederman, J., & Gunawardene, S. (2003). Does stimulant therapy of attention-deficit/hyperactivity disorder beget later substance abuse? A meta-analytic review of the literature. *Pediatrics, 111*, 179–85.

Zylowska, L., Ackerman, D., Yang, M., Futrell, N., Horton, N., Hale, T. S., . . . Smalley, S. (2008). Mindfulness meditation training in adults and adolescents with ADHD: A feasibility study. *Journal of Attention Disorders, 11*, 737–746.

Index

Index

Index

Index

Index

Index

About the Author

Patricia O. Quinn, MD, is a developmental pediatrician in Washington, DC. Dr. Quinn is a well-known international speaker and conducts workshops about AD/HD nationwide. She has authored several best-selling and groundbreaking books on AD/HD including *Attention, Girls! A Guide to Learn All About Your AD/HD* and with co-author Theresa Maitland, PhD, *Ready for Take-Off: Preparing Your Teen With ADHD or LD for College* and *On Your Own: A College Readiness Guide for Teens With ADHD/LD*. In 2000, Dr. Quinn received the CHADD Hall of Fame Award for her work in the field of AD/HD.